D0600521

OUTSIDE
ARCHITECTURE

ROCKPORT

DEDICATION

To my "big" sister and best

friend, Barbara Zevon Berlin,

with enormous gratitude for

her help with this book and

all things, always, I lovingly

dedicate this book.

OUTSIDE
ARCHITECTURE

*Outdoor Rooms
Designed by Architects*

Susan Zevon

GLOUCESTER MASSACHUSETTS

ROCKPORT
PUBLISHERS

Copyright © 1999 by Susan Zevon
First paperback edition printed in 2002

All rights reserved. No part of this book may be reproduced in any form without
written permission of the copyright owners. All images in this book have been
reproduced with the knowledge and prior consent of the artists concerned and no
responsibility is accepted by producer, publisher, or printer for any infringement of
copyright or otherwise, arising from the contents of this publication. Every effort
has been made to ensure that credits accurately comply with information supplied.

First published in the United States of America by
Rockport Publishers, Inc.
33 Commercial Street
Gloucester, Massachusetts 01930-5089
Telephone: (978) 282-9590
Facsimile: (978) 283-2742
www.rockpub.com

ISBN 1-56496-882-0

10 9 8 7 6 5 4 3 2 1

Design: Wren Design, Philadephia, PA
Front cover photograph: Pasture House, by Max Levy. Photo by Scott Frances,
    courtesy of *House Beautiful.*
Back cover photographs: (top) Walter Chatam loft, Photo by Kari Haavisto,
    courtesy of *House Beautiful.* (bottom) La Colorada house by Ricardo
    Legorreta, photo by Lourdes Legorreta.

Printed in China

Susan Zevon is a passionate devotee of architecture and a connoisseur of
interior design. She has served as the architecture editor of *House Beautiful* for
more than a decade, has held editorial positions at *Self* and *House and Garden*
magazines, and has been a contributor to the home design sections of the *New
York Times* and the *New York Post.* Ms. Zevon is the author of *Inside
Architecture.*

ACKNOWLEDGMENTS

My work as an architecture editor has brought me to many wonderful houses, where very often the most pleasant rooms were those open to the outdoors. Whether an urban roof garden, a terrace overlooking a verdant valley, a waterside deck, or a minimal courtyard, these spaces enhanced my sense of being in a special place. So, even as I completed work on *Inside Architecture, Interiors by Architects* (Rockport Publishers, Inc., 1996) I began thinking about *Outside Architecture*. Fortunately, Rosalie Grattaroti, Rockport Publisher's savvy acquisitions editor, shared my enthusiasm for the idea. While *Inside Architecture* focuses exclusively on U.S. architects, Rosalie requested that *Outside Architecture* should also include international projects. I am therefore grateful for the cooperation of architects on several continents whose work enriches this book.

My thanks go as well to the U.S. architects who provided many glorious projects and interesting ideas, especially to Walter Chatham for his thoughtful introduction and for all the inspiration his work has provided over the years. I extend a special note of tribute to the memory of William Turnbull, whose untimely death occurred shortly after I started work on this book. His loss was all the more poignant to me because, more than any other architect I know, Bill had the ability to design outdoor spaces that make us feel at home in the landscape. Fortunately, his designs remain an inspiration and his talented partners, Mary Griffin and Eric Haesloop, continue the firm's work.

I am very grateful to the accomplished photographers whose images enhance these pages. Many of them are cherished colleagues with whom I have worked for many years and from whom I continue to learn. Special thanks to Erica Stoller, director of Esto. Her generosity, efficiency, and enthusiasm were a great help in making this book possible.

My thanks to Martha Wetherill at Rockport Publishers for guiding the book through the crucial initial and final stages. I am also indebted to my colleagues at *House Beautiful*; to our editor-in-chief Louis Gropp for his astute forewords to both *Inside Architecture* and this book. My thanks to him and to our managing editor, Deborah Martin, for generously granting permission for me to use photographs of projects I originally produced for the magazine.

My steadfast agent, Barbara Hogenson, and her assistant, Sarah Feider, have earned my great appreciation. Above all, I thank my dear family—without their love and encouragement nothing would be possible.

CONTENTS

FOREWORD

LOUIS OLIVER GROPP

Editor in Chief
House Beautiful

With the success of Susan Zevon's first book, *Inside Architecture*, it is not surprising that *House Beautiful's* architecture editor has followed it with a second volume, aptly named *Outside Architecture*. Just as her first effort chronicled the growing involvement of architects in interior design, this second book captures the enrichment of outdoor space as an extension of the built environment.

More than just traditional courtyards, terraces, and decks, in the hands of an accomplished architect the room beyond the room can immeasurably enhance and integrate a house and its grounds. Texas architects Ted Flato and David Lake link new and existing buildings with porches, breezeways, and tall walls, for example, literally redefining corridors. Their outside architecture is designed to permit the use of these spaces for living during most months of the year.

Spanish architect Alberto Campo Baeza permits his building materials to flow between the indoor and outdoor spaces, merging what were once two separate worlds into one marvelous whole. And no one who has experienced firsthand the work of the disciples of Charles Moore can forget the delightful way William Turnbull or Buzz Yudell extends his dwellings into the landscape with breezeways, arbors, trellises, gazebos, and other architectural conceits.

In his introduction, Walter Chatham notes that "outside architecture" has been with us from the beginning, in such enduring built forms as Egyptian temples or Roman atria, but the examples in this book show how much more of a contemporary residence is now essentially "outside."

Outside architecture has greatly transformed life as we live it today, making it more relaxed, more related to nature, and more liveable than ever before. Architects have understood this for some time, which is why many of the projects in this volume are part of the architecture that architects have created for themselves.

As Susan Zevon has followed their work as an editor at *House & Garden* and now at *House Beautiful*, where she has been responsible for the coverage of architecture for over a decade, she has become captivated by the outdoor rooms designed by her friends in the profession. We can only be grateful that she has chosen to take the time and the care to share that work with us.

INTRODUCTION

WALTER CHATHAM

What is "outside architecture" and how is it different from a garden? A garden can be made to be occupied and used, but it can also be designed simply to provide pleasing views from the interior of a building. "Outside architecture" is made to be occupied and enjoyed. It employs built and natural elements—columns, walls, trees, or hedges—to enclose and define space, to create a sense of being, of belonging, inside of something. Outside architecture occurs wherever a portion of a garden or exterior space creates the feeling of enclosure.

In the beginning there was Eden, a place where nature existed as perfection. There was no intervention by the human will to dominate, and none was needed. All gardens, large or small, formal or informal, are characterized by the willful intention of a designer who seeks to create a place of refuge where a controlled vision of nature can be contemplated and enjoyed. The earliest gardens were made to provide a protected environment for the household to grow food. They were practical, no-nonsense places. The orderly pursuit of agriculture made for organized arrangements of plants, which ultimately led to the development of gardens for pleasure. People realized that in a garden, a bit of water and shade created a place to enjoy while resting from their labors. Walls and other architectural elements began to define the separateness and security that characterize control over nature and the elements.

"Outside architecture" has been with us from the beginning of recorded history. The Egyptian temples enclosed vast roofless spaces; the Greek temples were more open than closed. The Roman atrium house is an early example of the use of outdoor rooms as an integral part of the residence. The Islamic paradise garden, usually a walled space adjacent to a building or in a courtyard, was thought to be a literal evocation of the joys that await the pious in the afterlife. This concept of the outdoor room came to European culture through the returning crusaders, who told tales of the refreshing gardens of the holy land. The medieval cloisters adapted this concept to the wet, temperate northern climate. Monks and nuns, celebrating the wonder of creation in great outdoor rooms, tended elaborate mixes of flowers, fruits, and vegetables. The very nature of the monastery required that these spaces be separate from the temporal world beyond.

The gardens of the Orient, which are increasingly studied and appreciated in the West, depended on juxtaposition and skillful arrangement of elements such as plantings, rocks, gravel, water, and wood for their qualities rather than on overwhelming scale. In the East, inside and outside have been much more closely linked than in the West. For example, the rooms of a traditional Japanese house opened to the garden through large sliding screens that allowed space to flow freely between the interior and exterior. The garden was a direct adjunct to the house, extending the living areas into nature. Interestingly, it is these gardens that have come to provide the best model for the small private paradises that predominate today.

With the development of the garden came the notion of status accorded to its owner. The garden is essentially a luxury, yet part of its historical popularity had to do with the fact that it was possible for anyone who owned a bit of ground to create one. People have historically tended to be somewhat competitive when it comes to gardens. The European aristocracy sought to project power through the formal manipulation of nature to create vast outdoor rooms. The long axial views from the great palaces made manifest the notion of dominion over the earth and expressed in literal terms the projection of political and economic power. Space was carved from the forest rather than enclosed between stone walls. The elaborate simulacrums of nature contrived in the English garden were in some ways subtler, more sophisticated versions of this same impulse.

The architect in the West had little role to play in making gardens until the garden came to be seen as an extension of buildings during the Enlightenment. Gardens became complex, and this complexity needed to be ordered and controlled. The same desire to express perfection through built form was extended outdoors and the results were often stiff, formal, and geometrically arranged.

It is really the evolution of democratic society that has brought the architect to the forefront of garden design and the making of outside architecture. Frank Lloyd Wright's designs, unlike the axial landscape architecture of Le Nôtre and Le Brun, were celebrations of the ideal of democracy exploding across the plains. When Wright "destroyed the box," he also destroyed the Western notion of separation of interior from exterior space. It is no accident that Wright was a student of oriental art and architecture. The Orient has always celebrated the garden as a spatial

extension of the building. Nature is viewed as a model of perfection to be shaped sympathetically, without domination. After Wright, the concept of "outdoor room" gained increasing credence. The evolution of design in places such as Los Angeles led to increasing interaction between inside and outside. The work of Richard Neutra and Rudolph Schindler, both refugee architects from Europe, excelled at blurring the distinctions between inside and outside. It is hard now to realize how radical it seemed fifty years ago when Neutra designed the first school with outdoor classrooms.

Today, we take it for granted that the concept of "outside" includes habitation and use. Examples of outdoor rooms in modern society include stadiums and ballparks, memorial gardens, and other exterior enclosures where space can be controlled to create a sense of containment. Most of these are based on the classical models that still define our understanding of spatial manipulation and control. The many fine examples of outdoor rooms included in this book represent the accumulated knowledge of history; yet they also reveal the infinite possibilities of our age to go beyond what was done in the past. Technology has given us dominion over the earth, yet has made it essential for us to look beyond the control of nature as the ultimate goal of building. It is once again possible to view nature as a benevolent force to be shaped without the former destructive will to dominate. We are free to create outdoor rooms for pleasure—as an antidote, perhaps, to the increasingly bland world we have created "inside."

WILLIAM TURNBULL
IN CASE OF RAIN

William Turnbull has left a legacy of buildings, particularly in northern California where he lived and practiced for most of his career, that are so appropriate to their landscape, they seem an extension of the surrounding terrain. He began designing his ecologically sensitive dwellings at a time when the International Style dominated the imaginations of the architecturally avant-garde, and their steel and glass boxes were popping up on manicured lawns and city streets across the nation. His first major work, the Sea Ranch condominium designed in 1963 to 1965 in collaboration with Charles Moore, Donlyn Lyndon, and Richard Whitaker, on the coast of Sonoma County, California, helped change the course of architecture in the United States. The Sea Ranch condominiums draw on the wood barns that stood on the site, a former sheep farm, to create structures that Turnbull compared to "wooden rocks." By adapting the local vernacular to create environmentally sensitive buildings, the Sea Ranch condominiums provided a prototype, not just for northern California, but for places as far away as the east and Florida coasts.

Turnbull's houses embrace nature so intimately that the outdoor spaces are often as habitable as the rooms enclosed with walls. Of the diminutive 640-square-foot (57.6-square-meter) house he designed for himself, his wife, architect Mary Griffin, and their two young sons, William and Andrew, Turnbull wrote, "It is architecture that is combined with landscape architecture in a manner to make the larger rooms out of doors. Charles Keeler is supposed to have defined California architecture for Bernard Maybeck as landscape design with occasional rooms in case of rain. So be it: that is what this house is."

The tiny house, constructed from windfall trees, in its simplicity, thrift, unpretentiousness, and most of all its ability to heighten its inhabitants' awareness of being in a special place, is the quintessential expression of Turnbull's architecture. Only 10 feet (3 meters) wide, the house is set between two fruit trees on the only flat piece of land on a 20-acre (8-hectare) hillside vineyard overlooking Mt. St. Helena and the Knight's Valley north to Geyser Peak. The house faces an old wash house, that was converted to a potting shed, across an 80-by-80-foot (24.4-by-24.4-meter) lawn.

In the mornings the boys often use the lawn as a playing field, and in the evenings, from time to time they pull out their sleeping bags to watch the big dipper hanging over the hill. When the moonshine is so bright that it casts shadows on the grass, they perhaps think that if their father could create a place as magical as this, he could also have hung the moon.

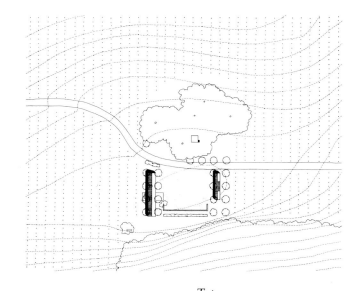

Top:
When open, a row of doors dissolves the boundary between indoor living space and the lawn.

Above:
Site Plan

Right:
For their wedding ceremony on the Vineyard, Griffin and Turnbull built a gazebo topped by two crosses made from plumbing pipe.

Below left:
A four-poster tree house set in a stand of mature oaks serves as a sleeping platform for the children. A claw-footed tub below provides outdoor bathing with a view of the mountain.

Below right:
A breezeway, with sliding glass and barn doors, serves as an open-air dining room.

Right:
The house is set on the one flat area of the hillside. Turnbull likened the surrounding vineyard with its geometric plantings to a formal French garden.

Left:
An old well house that was on the property when Turnbull bought it was converted into a potting shed.

Below:
Griffin tends her plants outside the potting shed.

CHARLES CORREA
BESTOWING THE BLESSINGS OF THE SKY

Charles Correa was born in Secunderabad, India. He was educated in the United States and is internationally recognized—the recipient of numerous awards and a sought-after teacher and lecturer worldwide. His practice is in his native India, where he has found the climate and architecture an inspiration, especially for the design of outdoor rooms. In his essay "The Blessings of the Sky," he writes:

> In India, the sky has profoundly affected our relationship to built form, and to open space. For in a warm climate, the best place to be in the late evenings and in the early mornings, is outdoors, under the open sky. . . . At each moment, subtle changes in the quality of light and ambient air generate feelings within us—feelings which are central to our beings. Hence to us in Asia, the symbol of education has never been the Little Red Schoolhouse of North America, but the guru sitting under the tree. True enlightenment cannot be achieved within the closed box of a room—one needs to be outdoors under the sky.

India's relatively benevolent climate makes outdoor living an almost year-round possibility. Correa finds in the buildings of his country an infinite variation of open-sky rooms: verandahs, terraces, and courtyards, often shaded by a tree or pergola. Whether designing a museum, resort, scientific institute, or government building, he tends to make outdoor rooms an ascendant theme in his architecture. They are integral to his residential work—multi-family housing as well as private villas. He recognizes their importance for the entire gamut of the population. For the poor they represent a much-needed extra room for cooking, visiting with friends, and sleeping at night. For the rich, terraces, courtyards, and open-air pavilions are as precious as their enclosed spaces.

Correa's designs often draw on the plan of the patio house, which is as traditional to India as to the Mediterranean. The old Hindu houses in Tami Nadu and Goa were, for example, organized around a small courtyard with a tree or Tulsi plant at its center. These shaded courtyards bring light and ventilation to the rooms that surround them. The central courtyard was pivotal to the design for his own house and studio in Bangalore, known as the House at Koramangala. Although the design kept changing during the construction process, the central courtyard remained constant, and he believes it was the courtyard "that allowed the rest to keep changing, right until the end."

Correa designed 38 villas on land along the Mandovi river across from the city of Panaji. Due to the elongated shape of the site, which runs between the road and the river bank, he strung the houses out so they all have a river view and a shared garden along the river. All of the villas at Verem have verandahs. In the house at the eastern end of the site that he uses as his own vacation villa, the living and dining areas are adjacent to an atrium. The rooms are cross-ventilated by the atrium, which he says "acts as a lung for the whole house."

Correa also provides outdoor rooms for the multi-family housing he designs. The Kanchanjunga apartments, a tower of thirty-two luxury condominiums in Bombay, completed in 1973, has deep, garden verandahs suspended in the air. More recently, he has been among four architects selected by an industrial unit in India to design housing for workers that is to be integral to new urbanization outside the small town of Hosur, near Bangalore. The plan, called Titan Township, includes shared and private gardens, as well as terraces and verandahs.

Correa believes that open-air spaces have metaphysical benefits, beyond their pragmatic functions. He writes about the mythic qualities of rooms open to the sky:

> The sky . . . is the source of light—which is the most primordial of stimuli acting on our senses. And across its face, every day, passes the sun—the origin of Life itself! . . . Small wonder then that man has always perceived the sky above to be the abode of the gods, and down all these many millennia, it has exerted such extraordinary power on us and on the architecture we build.

House at Koramangala
*Granite blocks may be used as
seats in the studio garden.*

*Below:
A champa tree grows in the
courtyard.*

The front door is placed off-center on the main façade. From it visitors move along a shifting axis to the courtyard.

Right:
A Doberman in the courtyard.

Burma teakwood doors, taken from the turn-of-the-century bungalow that was the architect's former residence, were hand-painted by him "to celebrate their new incarnation."

The courtyard seen through the
bamboo shades that separate it
from the interior rooms.

Villas at Verem
Below left:
A door with three flaps separates the living room from the terrace overlooking the river. The two upper flaps are painted with the scene of the river and surrounding landscape that one sees from the terrace. Here, the upper flap is shown partly open.

Below right:
Looking from just inside the living room across the verandah to the river.

Top:
Verandahs have a view across
the back garden to the river.

Below:
Inside the living room looking
toward the three-flap doors
that open the room to the river.

Kanchanjunga Apartments
Top:
The surface of the building is
cut away at the corners to open
double-height terrace gardens
at the corners.

Below:
View of the southeast elevation
of the tower within the context
of the city.

Top:
The surface of the building is cut away at the corners to create double-height terrace gardens.

Below:
On a terrace garden.

Titan Township
Top left:
Master Plan

Top right:
Site Plan

Below:
Section Drawing

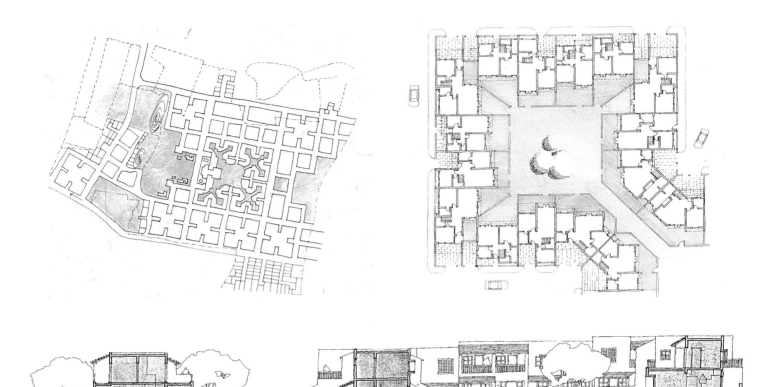

Top:
Model of a typical module showing how the houses are clustered around a back garden with verandahs and courtyards opening to the garden.

Below:
Elevation

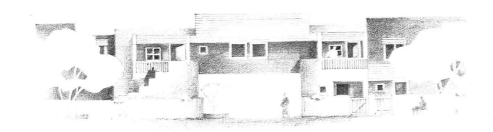

JAMES CUTLER
REVERING THE LAND

In his practice of architecture James Cutler reveres the land as part of the living universe. His passion for protecting the landscape governs his designs whether he is working on the 40,000-square-foot (3,600-square-meter) private compound in Medina, Washington, that he designed in collaboration with Peter Bohlin for Microsoft chairman Bill Gates, or his many more modest projects. "My profession is wanton in its destruction of trees," he says. "I save what I can, and I regret the ones I kill."

Soon after graduating from the University of Pennsylvania where he studied with Louis Kahn, Cutler moved to the Pacific Northwest where he now heads his own small firm on Bainbridge Island, Washington. He is one of a new generation of architects whose commitment to the environment is having a seminal effect on the relation between nature and construction. He hopes that the buildings he designs will make his clients more aware of their environment, and he regards outdoor rooms as special opportunities to provide close contact with nature.

> *Made outdoor spaces are very often tied to and extensions of interior architectural spaces. They are, however, if done well, more than servants to the architecture. They are places that remind us of our connection to everything else alive. In a way, outside spaces are the place of our primal memories of these connections and therefore provide a sense of well-being. . . . At their best they reveal the true nature of the living world, of which we are physically only a part.*

Cutler gave wonderful form to these beliefs in a modest, 2,300-square-foot (207-square-meter) house he designed for a retired couple on Washington State's Olympic Peninsula. Only three trees were felled in the construction of this house in a dense forest perched on a 200-foot (61-meter) bluff that overlooks Hood Canal. He anchored the house to the ground at its south end where 20-foot (6.1-meter) rhododendrons grow. As the ground falls away beneath it, the house floats out on stilts to 15 feet (4.6 meters) off the ground at its north end. A 127-foot (38.7-meter) bridge leads from the driveway through the rhododendrons to the front door and continues for 48 feet (14.6 meters) out the back, floating on stilts over the brow of the bank and ending with a deck that offers a view of the water beneath the shade of alders. He has choreographed the movement through the house so that its owners and their guests experience the beauty of the forest. "If you learn to love the trees, you are bound to protect them," he says. "It is a wonderful feeling to know you are part of a larger living organism."

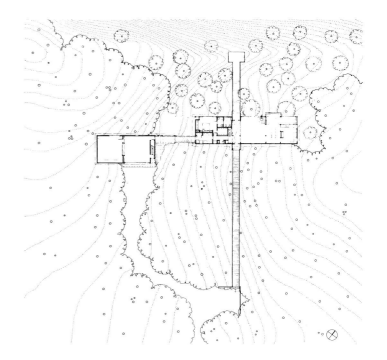

Top:
Site plan

Above:
View of the entry bridge from inside the front door.

Right:
A dining deck under the eaves.

Top left:
Visitors follow the cedar entrance bridge flanked by rhododendrons from the driveway to the front door.

Top Right:
The entry bridge spans 127 feet (38.7 meters) from the driveway to the front door.

Below:
The walkway that leads from the back of the house to the water.

Right:
The back deck ends with a small platform that offers a view of the water. The land beneath the bridge was carefully cleared by machete.

HUGH NEWELL JACOBSEN
OUTDOOR REFLECTIONS

Houses on several continents that defer to their surroundings stand as proof of Hugh Newell Jacobsen's conviction that "good architecture like a well bred lady does not shout at her neighbors." After a short apprenticeship in the offices of Philip Johnson and Keys Lethbridge and Condon, Jacobsen established his own firm in Washington, D.C., building a distinguished international practice predominantly from residential work. His designs are at once classical abstractions of the local vernacular and clearly recognizable as his work. A Jacobsen house is distinguished by the clarity of its plan, the precision of its proportions, and the exaltation of the landscape. His larger houses are typically divided into a series of linked pavilions, with the spaces between the buildings as carefully designed as the interior rooms. The outdoor rooms often reflect the proportions of the interiors. "I have found that the terrace addressing the house and the garden is most pleasing to the eye and in use, as well, when it is the same dimensions as the interior space it serves," he says. "This reflection in plan is a subtle memory overlay and establishes the necessary order." Frequently he uses the same flooring material inside and out, so the outdoor rooms appear to continue the enclosed space.

Jacobsen's own house is located in the historic Georgetown section of Washington, D.C., just a few blocks from his office. "The garden," he says, "is the magic of a Georgetown house." A library adjacent to the living room shares the view of the garden, which reflects the proportions of the two interior rooms. For his urban garden he created a stone terrace that extends to a bank of ivy stretching toward two matching rows of columnar American holly trees planted along the back garden wall. "Cool and evergreen, the trees are individually lit at night to erase interior reflections on the 10-foot-high (3.0-meter-high) sections of glass," he explains. This house was the first project in which he employed his now familiar floor-to-ceiling openings between rooms, without moldings or baseboards. There is nothing to interrupt the eye as it is drawn to the view of the garden.

Jacobsen's mastery of vernacular abstraction is as apparent in his outdoor rooms as in the modeling of his buildings. The playful juxtaposition of indoor and outdoor rooms in the two houses he designed in the Dominican Republic typify resort architecture. The house designed in 1987 near the town of La Romana is composed of seven pavilions linked by sun-screened passages and courtyards open to the sky. A white travertine-like marble quarried on the island and left unpolished covers all the floors, inside and out, enhancing the flow of rooms out to the breezeways and terraces. The composition of another house in the Dominican Republic completed two years later grew to twelve pavilions, including a tropical living room, eighty-percent open to the sea air.

For the design of a house in an overgrown nineteenth-century garden in Holland, Jacobsen abstracted the stepped gables of sixteenth- and seventeenth-century houses in nearby Dutch villages. A pond reflects the house, and in plan a series of terraces mirror the proportions of the interior rooms. The living room extends across a terrace with the same dimensions toward the view of the pond. Two step-gabled wings flank a skylit dining room and protect the adjoining dining terrace from the wind. The master bedroom opens to its own terrace.

In Windsor, a new community in Florida, Jacobsen designed a vacation house with a backyard almost totally composed of a brilliant blue swimming pool that stretches from the outside edge of the living room to a pavilion designed for relaxing after a swim and leisurely poolside meals. "Water is a great architectural tool," he says. "Its reflections add mystery and romance to a building."

High above the plain of Attica, where the modern city of Athens sprawls below the ancient Acropolis, Jacobsen, working with an Athenian colleague, Andreas Simeon, designed a house built into a steep slope of solid rock. Long white marble terraces act as sun screens for the interior rooms whose glass walls face out toward the historic plain. The colonnaded terraces recall ancient Greek temples. A swimming pool surrounded by a terrace and sun pavilion is carved into the rock. When the sun sets, the fluted columns rising from the long parallel terraces frame the light that shines through the glass walls across the plain toward Marathon.

House in Georgetown, Washington, D.C.
View of the garden from the library of the Jacobsen house. "The garden is designed as a room, an extension of the house," says the architect.

A white awning shades a dining table on the stone terrace in the garden. Fifteen columnar American holly trees are planted in two matching rows at the rear of the garden.

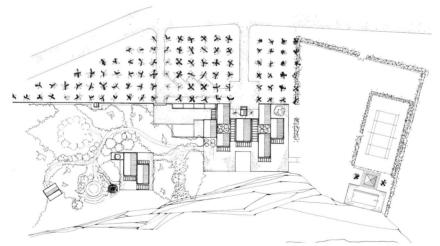

House in Dominican Republic near La Romana
Top left:
The pavilioned house seen through a coconut grove. The house rests on a podium surfaced with white, travertine-like marble.

Above:
Site Plan

Top right:
The "master's" house, removed from the main house by 200 feet (64 meters) echoes the same architecture.

Right:
One of the two sun-screened passages that join the living room pavilion with others. On the right, the dining room with three exposures to the outdoors.

Following pages:
Twilight view from the living room looking across the pool and adjoining terraces to the sea.

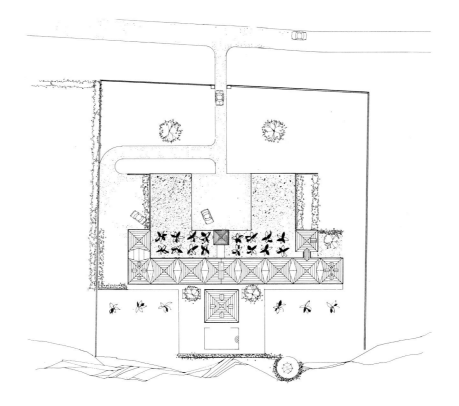

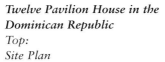

Twelve Pavilion House in the Dominican Republic
Top:
Site Plan

Above left:
View toward the sea with the living room pavilion on the right.

Above right:
A dining table shaded by a white awning on the terrace.

Right:
The dining pavilion with sliding louvered walls open to the view of the sea.

House in Windsor, Florida
left:
At twilight the pavilion is reflected in the pool, seen from inside the living room. The pool pavilion, Jacobsen says, "is a mirrored elevation of the living room without the sash."

Below left:
A pool flanked by two terraces stretches from the house to the pavilion.

Below right:
The pavilion provides a shelter from the sun and a pleasant place for meals.

House in the Netherlands
View of the house from across the private pond. The largest terraces are on the water's edge.

Below:
Site Plan

Right:
The glazed, tree-lined entrance hall serves as an interior "street."

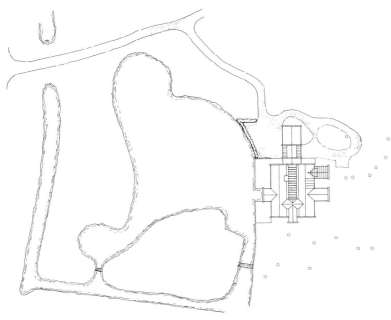

House in Athens, Greece
Below:
The house steps down a rocky
cliff. The pool is four levels
below the entrance level.

Bottom left:
The pavilion near the pool
is shaded by a sun screen
supported by the fluted columns
repeated throughout the house.

Bottom right:
View of the upper levels of the
house from across the pool,
with the colonnaded terraces on
the right.

Right:
The twilight view of the long
white marble terrace, looking
north. A corner of the living
room is seen on the left.

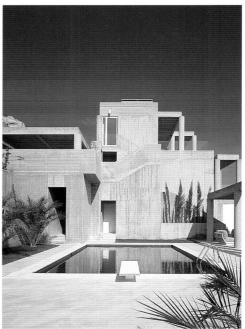

MAX LEVY
THE PROMISE OF SHADE

Under the big sky of the Lone Star State the porch is a promise of shade. Max Levy, who heads his own architectural firm in Dallas, cannot imagine designing a house without a "significant" porch. "The porch," he explains, "is the first step out of the cave. It is powerful because, like the hearth, it is primal. People have instinctual needs that are thwarted by modern life. One of them is to linger—to be alive, yet still and calm." He believes that the porch is one of the few places left where you can do that.

On a sliver of land locked between a creek and a six-lane highway, Levy created an oasis of calm for a doctor, dancer, and their young son. Zooming along the highway you might totally miss this house, peeping discreetly above its brick wall, were it not for the bright yellow awning propped above it. This welcoming banner, the color of sunshine, shades a skylit porch designed as a separate pavilion between the building that contains a large studio, kitchen, and dining area and a smaller building that encloses the bedrooms. The awning prevents the porch from being clobbered by the hot Texas sun, but because the fabric is fifty-percent open, it allows you to see the clouds through it. The color casts a glow that makes the room seem sunny even on the occasional gray day. A long tiled gallery connects the three pavilions. The plant-filled screened porch opens only to the gallery, not to the outdoors. "I wanted to keep it from becoming a vestibule," Levy explains. It is a place to see the trees and listen to the sound of the creek, a space in which to linger and be calm.

Some years later, Levy designed a house on pasture land on the fringe of Dallas for a woman in her eighties who is a painter and poet. "On the prairie's uneventful landscape, every wildflower becomes a jewel and the most interesting thing is the sky," Levy says, so he focused the house on the sky. The primal ideas of porch and hearth are combined into a cylindrical screened porch that is open to the sky on top. "By framing the sky," he says, "our awareness becomes focused. It has the soothing quality of an ocean view." On chilly fall and spring evenings the fireplace prolongs the time when the porch can be used.

The porch is on a dog trot that connects the 24-by-35-foot (7.3-by-10.7-meter) loft-like living space to a separate building that contains a studio and guest quarters. The loft's flat roof is punctuated by skylights that give each of the principal living spaces a carefully framed sky view. A steel staircase that rises diagonally in front of the screened porch leads to the roof where the skylights are topped by shading devices so that the house does not get beaten by the sun. The owner loves to go up to the roof at night to watch the stars. When the moonlight shimmers on the roof's white surface and she wanders amidst the pyramidal shapes of the skylights, she feels like she is in Egypt.

"Celebrating the wind, sky, and rain give a new life to modernism," Levy says. His outdoor rooms connect their inhabitants with the Texas landscape in a way that gives regionalism a more profound significance.

Ceiling fans stir up a breeze inside the plant-filled screened porch.

Highway House
Top left:
Screened from the din of a
Dallas highway by a brick wall
and windowless façade, the
house consists of three small
pavilions, one of which
encloses a screened porch.

Bottom left:
At night the awning glows
above the street like a lantern.

Top right:
Levy placed the pavilions so that
they "tiptoe around the trees."

Bottom right:
Close-up view of the awning-
topped skylight above the porch.

Sky House
Top:
Inside the screened porch,
chaises face the fireplace.

Below left:
A gravel pathway leads from
one end of a garden to the
reflecting pool.

Below right:
A metal staircase reaches up to
the roof.

Top:
A stone path stretches across the
back of the house where concrete
walls extend out into the prairies
to enclose the cultivated gardens.
"The stone-enclosed pool anchors
the structure to the earth,"
says Levy.

Below:
The screened cylindrical porch
of this house is situated on a
dog trot between the living
space and the studio.

Following pages:
At night the porch is reflected
in the pool.

TADAO ANDO
ABSTRACTING NATURE

Born in Japan in 1941, Tadao Ando has achieved worldwide preeminence. Self-educated, he studied architecture by visiting buildings—the temples, shrines, and tea houses in Kyoto and Nara—and by reading. With money he earned as a boxer, he traveled to the United States, Europe, and Africa between 1962 and 1969. When he returned to Japan he founded Tadao Ando Architect & Associates in Osaka. During the 1990s Ando's international reputation has been acknowledged by winning the Carlsberg Award for Architecture in Denmark, the Pritzker Prize, which has been called the Nobel Prize for architecture, the Praemium Imperiale given by the brother of the Emperor of Japan, and the Royal Institute of British Architects' Gold Medal. He is the only living architect to have received all four of these major architecture prizes.

Ando's buildings are memorable for the power of their restraint and the almost mystical way in which he introduces light and nature into their simple geometric forms. He says, "I believe that when greenery, water, light, or wind is abstracted from nature-as-is according to man's will, it approaches the sacred." This belief is a fundamental theme of his architecture, whether he is designing a church or residence. All his houses have courtyard gardens that are intrinsic to their plan. He writes: "In the courtyard, nature presents a different aspect of itself each day. The courtyard is the nucleus of life that unfolds within the house and is a device to introduce light, wind, and rain that are being forgotten in the city. By introducing nature and changing light into simple geometric forms that are closed off from their urban contexts, I create complex spaces."

Ando first gained recognition with the design of the Azuma house, a small row house in the Sumiyoshi district of his native Osaka. Built in a crowded, bustling neighborhood, the house is concealed behind a simple concrete façade broken only by the rectangular entrance. Inside, the rooms are organized around an interior courtyard. On the first floor French doors open the living room to the court. Across the courtyard is the kitchen/dining room. A stairway on one side of the courtyard rises to the upper level where two bedrooms, one for the adults, the other for the children, are connected by a concrete bridge that spans the distance between them. Thus one can go from one room to another only by going outside. While on a practical level this might be considered inconvenient, it exemplifies one of the great themes of Ando's approach to architecture. "I inject the extraordinary into what is the most ordinary and familiar of environments—the house—and thereby encourage people to

reconsider what is ordinary," he says. By making it a necessity for the inhabitants to step outside he brings them constantly into direct contact with sun, wind, light, and shadow—the elements of nature that may be forgotten in urban life. He considers the Azuma House the point of origin for all his subsequent work.

Years later, in his design for the Kidosaki house, a three-family house designed for an architect, his wife, and their parents in a quiet residential suburb of Tokyo, Ando inserted terraces and courtyards into the plan to connect the living quarters. These concrete-walled outdoor rooms provide spaces for companionship among the family members and introduce light, wind, and rain into daily living as the courtyard does in the Azuma house.

More recently, in designing the Nomi house, a two-family town house in downtown Osaka, Ando devoted roughly the same volume to outdoor and indoor living spaces. A two-story concrete wall completely encloses the two-household home, providing privacy. The two bedrooms on the ground level each open to a private courtyard. The living, dining areas and a terrace are reached by a staircase just beyond a single opening in the wall surrounding the perimeter of the property.

Ando writes that in the traditional Japanese row house, "each courtyard creates its own quiet, calm, and miniature universe into which abstractly generated nature penetrates." He has endowed his own buildings with the same presence of time symbolized by the constant changes in the light, climate, plants, and birds in his quest to "express a living architecture."

Azuma House
Above:
Axonometric

Right:
The central courtyard of the Azuma house is open to the sky. On the ground level it connects the living room to the kitchen, dining room, and bathroom on the other side. A staircase leads to the second level where a bridge connects the two bedrooms.

Kidosaki House
Below left:
Aerial view shows how the protective wall along the property line ends in a quarter-circle arc that curves inward from the street to lead visitors inside.

Below middle:
Floor Plans

Below right:
Just beyond the curved entry wall are staircases that lead to the apartments.

Below bottom right:
To maintain continuity with the land, Ando planted the same variety of trees in the courtyards that formerly grew on the site.

Right:
A view of one of the courtyard gardens that connects the living spaces occupied by three families.

Nomi House
Below left:
Site Plan

Below middle:
Floor Plans
Section
Axonometric

Below right:
In this two-family house each
of the bedrooms on the ground
level has its own courtyard.

Right:
Ando planted a large Zelkova
tree in the rear courtyard "to
watch over the occupants of the
house and provide a token
dialogue with the green of the
neighboring homes."

Following pages:
A terrace expands the living
spaces on the second level.

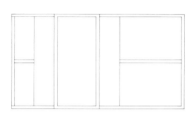

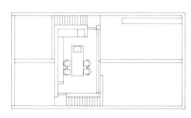

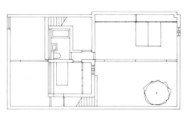

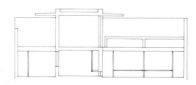

ANTOINE PREDOCK
ICONS IN THE LANDSCAPE

Antoine Predock believes that every site has a story. Limestone outcroppings, a mountain in the desert, even a kidney-shaped pool in a backyard are all iconic references that affect his designs. "When I am working on projects with my team . . . we remind ourselves that we are involved in a timeless encounter with another place, not just a piece of land," he says. Although best known for the adobe buildings he has designed in New Mexico, where he has been principal of his own firm in Albuquerque since 1967, his commissions have spanned the country from Saratoga Lake, New York to Southern California.

Integral to his work is his belief that outdoor space and architecture are one thing. Well known as an architect, Predock is also a licensed landscape architect. His interest in dance has also had a profound influence on his work. "I think of my buildings as processional events, as choreographic events; they are an accumulation of vantage points both perceptual and experiential," he writes. He designs to heighten people's awareness of the environment as they move through the rooms, both inside and out. A house on the outskirts of Phoenix, Arizona, for example, follows the course of the sun with a "sunrise" terrace positioned at its east end and a "sunset" tower that faces west. The daytime and evening wings of the house are united by a loggia bordering a large courtyard with a central pool. The pool collects water that runs through a channel parallel to the east-west axis of the house, as well as water issuing from boulders that climb up to define the beamed perimeter of the courtyard.

For a house outside Phoenix on the south-facing slope of Mummy Mountain with a sweeping view of the valley from which Camelback Mountain rises, Predock grouped the interior rooms around a series of semi-enclosed courtyards. A steel bridge that serves as both an entrance gateway and a terrace is aimed for viewing local flight patterns. "It is a bridge that goes anywhere and nowhere," he says. "It will take you as far as your imagination will travel." A series of different water gardens enhance his image of the house as an oasis in the desert.

Water often plays a key role in Predock's designs. For a house in Venice Beach, California, with the Pacific Ocean in its backyard, Predock says he directed the house "relentlessly" toward the sea, "by setting up a series of vantage points . . . that have to do only with the ocean and the imagined realms beyond." An 8-by-14-foot (2.4-by-4.3-meter) window wall at the building's west end pivots to open the house to the sound of the surf and breezes that carry the scent of the salty water. Predock had the giant window frame painted red to signal the color of the Chinese flag across the ocean.

On property six blocks from the Pacific in Manhattan Beach, California, Predock tore down an existing shack, but preserved a palm tree and kidney-shaped pool in the backyard as "icons" of the site, recollections of the property's more casual beginnings. The house he designed there has a deck at mid-level that faces the ocean. A third floor aerie, open to the sky, is sometimes used for dance performances under the stars.

While Predock's buildings now span the country, he has found that the lessons he learned designing in New Mexico can be implemented anywhere. "I think of it as a force that has entered my system," he writes. "Here one is aimed toward the sky and at that same time remains rooted in the earth with a geological and cultural past." A clear expression of this belief is a house he calls "Theater of the Trees," which he designed for clients in Dallas who are enthusiastic bird watchers. Large limestone ledges at the entrance to the house recall the building's relationship to the site. Almost every room has access to outdoor spaces. The roof itself is used as a viewing platform, and a dramatic metal-framed sky ramp juts over a ravine through the surrounding canopy of trees toward the sky.

House near Phoenix
The house is set against a range of rocky hills, and faces across a valley with metropolitan Phoenix at its center. Morning and evening areas of the house are linked by a central courtyard.

A loggia lines the courtyard to the left of the pool.

Below left:
*Stairs lead up to the sunrise
pavilion to the left of the
entrance to the house.*

Below right:
Site Plan

Right:
*A fountain in front of the
sunrise pavilion near the entry.*

Inside the sunset tower, accessible only through the master bedroom, light passing through the painted steel trellis casts a pattern on the stucco walls.

Water flows into the pool from a channel that emerges from within the house to meet a stream that flows into the pool from the boulders on the right side of the courtyard.

At dawn the pyramid-shaped
study glows in the courtyard.
The sunset tower is to the left.

WILKINSON LIBRARY
TELLURIDE,CO 81435

House on Mummy Mountain

Left:
Looking into the den from the courtyard over the fountain with the master bedroom above.

Below left:
The front entrance of the house at sunset, with the steel bridge that is both entrance gateway and viewing terrace.

Bottom left:
Site Plan

Below right:
At night, the bridge lit from below resembles an airport runway.

Middle right:
The main entry to the house.

Bottom right:
Looking out from the entry foyer to the reflecting pool.

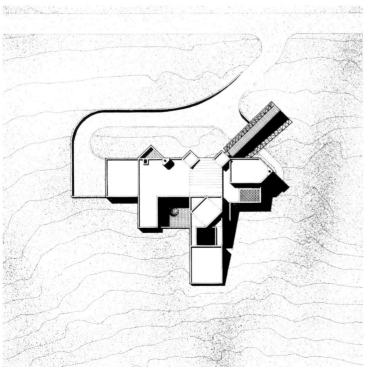

House in Venice Beach
Top left:
Passers-by on the boardwalk in back of the house.

Bottom left:
Floor Plans

Bottom right:
The house is focused toward the ocean. In the living room an 8-by -14 foot (2.4- by- 4.3 meter) aperture rotates on roller bearings to open the house to the sea.

Right:
A gray granite monolith under a film of recirculated water when viewed from inside the house seems to dissolve the space between the house and the ocean.

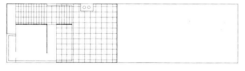

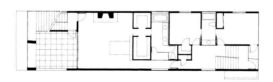

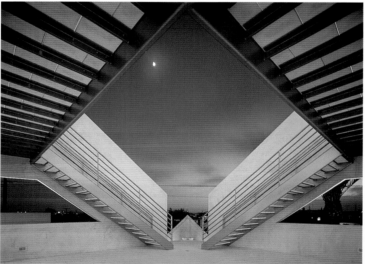

House in Manhattan Beach
Top:
Predock preserved a kidney-shaped pool and palm tree on the site, in a courtyard with doors that open to the living/dining room. Concrete steps lead up to a raised garden. The steel staircase on the right climbs up to an inner courtyard.

Above:
Twilight view of the steel-and-concrete-stairs that extend from the mid-level deck that faces the ocean.

At night the upper level glows like a lantern above the terrace, where dance performances are sometimes held under the stars.

Theater of the Trees
Top left:
At the entrance to this house in Dallas, Texas, called Theater of the Trees, Predock says "giant lime-stone ledges create a weighty and earthbound foreground: a dam of expectations." They are made of the material found in the Austin Chalk Formation, which runs through Dallas. The ledges are filled with plants to attract birds.

Bottom left:
The sky ramp extends past the cylindrical dining tower over a sloped ravine.

Top right:
A black steel sky ramp projects from the entry foyer into the canopy of trees.

Bottom right:
The skylight on the roof terrace above the dining room.

Right:
Predock says that the sky ramp's "predominantly tensile-steel composi-tion resonates with the wind, like an instrument, blending with the music of the birds." It extends up from a concrete prow toward Turtle Creek.

PETER MCMAHON AND SUSAN JENNINGS

SERVING NATURE

During six summers Peter McMahon and Susan Jennings built a vacation house that grew out of their love for the Cape Cod landscape. It was designed to enhance contact with nature and to respect the cape's fragile ecology. They succeeded with the guidance of a book they took out from the Boston Public Library, titled *How to Build Your Vacation House*; with the help of friends, and with a mere $25,000, which included a new septic system. The project was blessed with the enormous inventiveness and perseverance of its designers. Both were trained as architects but have also at times pursued other careers—McMahon as a furniture designer and teacher of architectural design, archaeology, drawing, and map-making in New York City public high schools; and Jennings as an artist and designer.

Their inspiration came from the summer homes in the vicinity created by such architectural luminaries as Eero Saarinen and Marcel Breuer, and by local architects like Charlie Zender. It also came from the Cape's tradition of being a place where artists and designers have gathered to relax and pursue their crafts. The house was put together mostly from scavenged building materials. The steel windows were "intercepted" as they were being discarded from a printing plant in Hoboken, New Jersey. The bathtub and sinks were salvaged by friends; the furnishings were designed and made by Peter and supplemented with finds from the Truro and Wellfleet dumps. All the art was made by Peter and Susan or donated by family and friends.

To preserve the flora and fauna and to raise the building above the flood plain, they built it on six concrete columns a few feet above the ground. Only one small tree was removed from the site; others were incorporated into the structure. McMahon and Jennings created the house to be at once sheltering and open to nature. A fir deck wraps around two sides. A wall of windows extends along the southeast façade, opening the main room to the view of the treetops. This room was designed specifically for an annual performance party; the rest of the time it serves as a living room and studio. The second room is a sleeping porch, screened on two sides, yet protected from the rain by an aluminum roof that McMahon says "curves over protectively like an overturned boat on the beach." The house protects them from the weather and insects but is bathed in salt, sand, and sunshine and the sounds of birds and waves washing the beach. Jennings writes:

A porch for sleeping is architecture subservient to nature. On Cape Cod, lying in an outdoor bed and awaiting sleep, one can watch a dance of rustling branches against a background of stars unbelievably numerous. Or take in the light from the rising full moon washed over skin and furniture as the sounds of night enter the dream state. . . . Far off waves continuously crash on the shore with a steady lulling. Always the air is salty, soft, and good as it is breathed with the rhythm of deep sleep. Sometimes the wonderful sounds of rain mingle with drowsiness. Water drops hit leaves with a pat-pat and fall on the bed of pine needles below, releasing soft smells of earth. Each morning the dramatic first light comes, always a surprise, as if it had been forgotten that darkness was not permanent.

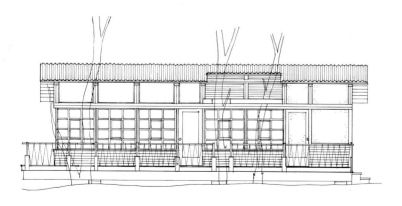

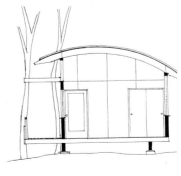

House on Cape Cod
Far left:
Southeast elevation

Left:
Section

Right:
Only one small tree was removed from the site to build the house. Others are embraced by the structure.

Previous pages:
Doors open to the deck, which is shaded by the overhang of the curved roof and by the treetops.

Top:
The house, raised on concrete piers, reaches up toward the treetops. A fir deck extends around two sides.

Above left:
Inside the sleeping porch, the structural spruce planks beneath the curved aluminum roof are exposed.

Above right:
Detail of the deck railing made from galvanized plumbing pipe and boating rope.

Right:
At night the interior space glows through the wall of windows and the screened sleeping porch.

BATTER KAY ASSOCIATES
TRANSPARENT ROOMS

"In Southern California," says Michael Batter, "because of the moderate climate, people spend as much time outdoors as indoors, so we try to create a transparency between indoor and outdoor space." This is particularly practical in the coastal regions, where their Del Mar-based firm has designed many houses, because building sites tend to be small. The architects are able to create larger living volumes by using the indoor/outdoor relationship.

Batter and Janice Kay met while they were attending the Harvard Graduate School of Design. After graduation Janice returned to her native Southern California, where Michael joined her a few years later to form the architectural firm Batter Kay Associates. Initially by chance, later by choice, their practice has been for the most part residential, resulting in numerous award-winning houses on the California coast.

In their early houses the outdoor spaces tended to be extensions of the interior floor plans. With time, their designs for outdoor spaces have evolved into rooms with walls that extend into the landscape. Walls not only define and enclose the spaces, but serve to provide privacy from roads and neighboring houses and protection from the sun.

"The site breeds the excitement of the plan," says Batter. It was the site that dictated the formation of the outdoor spaces of the first house designed by Batter Kay. The house is placed toward the top of a hill facing the ocean. Walls from a lap pool dug into the side of the hill help retain the earth. Stairs that also serve as seats step up from the pool to a terrace in back of the house with windbreaks and outdoor sculpture. The architects were so proud of this first project, built on speculation, that when a potential buyer proposed changing the design, they decided to barter their design services in order to buy the house themselves from their financial partner. Janice and Michael were married in the house, and have lived in it ever since, adding on to the outdoor space as their family has grown.

Several years later they designed another house in Del Mar, also on a hill. Here the house faces the ocean across a busy street. The house, called Seaview, steps down the hillside to give each room an ocean view. Layered walls that define the interior spaces extend out into the landscape to provide privacy for the outdoor rooms.

For a country estate set into an orange grove on a hilltop with a 270-degree view of the surrounding Southern California landscape, Batter Kay used concrete columns to order the interior and outdoor spaces of the pool, tennis court, and pool house that they created for the estate. "The columns that march through the interior of the house continue marching along the edge of the pool and are used for a lattice/sun screen that attaches to the pool/guest house," Batter explains.

A couple for whom Batter Kay had already designed a main residence in Southern California asked them to do a weekend retreat in the Napa Valley that would fit right in with the forest, open to the outdoors and yet be secure when they were away. Inspired by the old wine storage sheds that dot the landscape, they designed a house of three small parts, painted the color of the Pacific Madrone trees and framed by the tall trunks. Garage-type doors roll up to reveal a roofless courtyard between the main house and guest quarters. "We love the way the house enables us to move from inside to outside as though the spaces were one," says the husband. The owners of other Batter Kay houses would agree.

Batter Kay House
The first house designed by Batter Kay—later to become their own home—has a lap pool carved into the side of the hill. Steps lead up to a sitting area.

Top:
A hilltop terrace in back of
the house has a seating area
protected by a wall. Concrete
lounge and table inspired by
Le Corbusier.

Above left:
"Modular Man," a metal
sculpture the architects created
in homage to Le Corbusier,
stands on the lawn across from
the ocean.

Above right:
Concrete cylinders for viewing
the ocean are placed at the top
of the site, in front of the swing
and terrace.

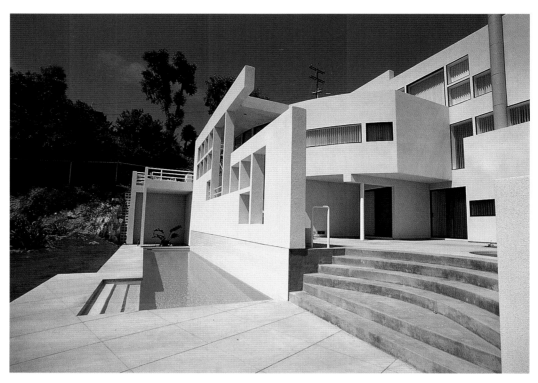

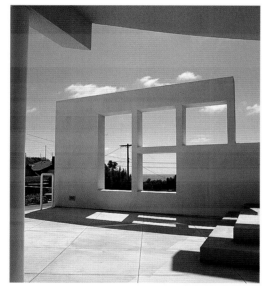

Seaview House

Top:
The house has a lap pool with a viewing deck above. A wall that rises from the pool screens the house.

Above left:
The wall frames the ocean view and screens the house from the noise and view of passers-by on the street.

Above right:
The spa is screened by a curved wall.

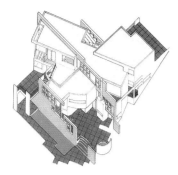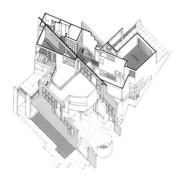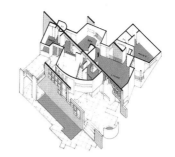

Top:
Cut-away axonometric
drawings showing plans at
each level.

Above:
Steps behind the wall that
extends along the lap pool lead
up to the interior of the house.

Villa Lago
Top:
Concrete columns along the
pool extend from the interior
space outside.

Below left:
Looking across the pool to
the house.

Below right:
Detail of the pool and the
wall that separates it from the
tennis court.

Top:
Stairway steps down from the pool to the tennis court and provides seating for viewing the matches.

Below left:
Columns mark off an outdoor room between the house, pool house, and tennis court.

Below right:
Cut-away axonometric

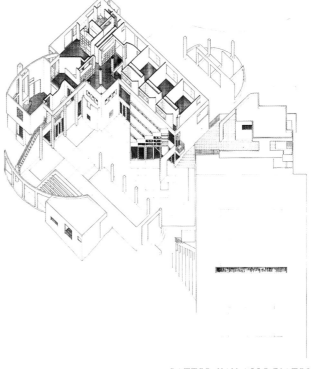

Napa Valley Retreat
Painted the color of the Pacific
Madrone trees, this weekend
retreat in the Napa Valley is
designed as three small buildings
that are framed by the tall trunks.

Right:
The courtyard extends the
living room and guest room to
the outdoors.

Top:
The main house is raised above a garage, and a bridge connects it to a spa in its own small tower.

Above left:
View of the courtyard from the guest bedroom.

Above right:
Detail of the deck looking toward the spa.

Top left:
View of the deck from inside
the house.

Top right:
Garage type doors roll up to
reveal the roofless courtyard.

Above:
The owners turn on the
fountain in the courtyard each
morning before enjoying
breakfast under an umbrella
set among the trees.

ELIZABETH DEMETRIADES
A FOREGROUND FOR NATURE

"Outside architecture," says Elizabeth Demetriades, "creates scale in the context of site—be it an expansive backdrop of horizon or a tapestry of tree lines, rock outcroppings, and hillsides. Sculptural forms become the foreground for natural elements and establish a dialogue with them." Her architectural practice has been indelibly linked to the landscape since 1988, when, just two years after establishing an independent architecture office in New York City, she began a land development corporation to create protected land subdivisions and build speculative houses on 400 acres (160 hectares) of farmland in New York State's Columbia County while maintaining the agricultural use of the fields by the local dairy farmers.

Soon afterwards, in response to numerous residential commissions in the area, she moved her firm to Ancramdale, New York. The firm's work grew to include projects throughout New York State and northwestern Connecticut. In 1996 Demetriades opened an office in New York City in joint venture with Patrick Walker Designs, while still maintaining her country practice. The firm's work includes both traditional and modern design. "The choreography of light, volume, and spatial progression transgresses the limits of stylistic labels," she says.

When clients in rural Connecticut requested a place to enjoy swimming and tennis "separate in location and spirit from their rather traditional home," Demetriades designed a pool house about 200 feet (61 meters) from the existing house in a sloping field facing south. A wedge-shaped retaining wall conceals the pool area from view except for a quick glimpse that is allowed through an opening in the wall. Twelve steps along the southern face of the wall lead through a shaded cloister area to the pool. A stand of tall oaks and maples provides a lush green backdrop for the small building from where one looks south across the pool to the sky.

Demetriades used materials that emphasize the play of light and shadow on the exterior surfaces and lend a surprising poetry to the simple geometric forms. A steel-framed curved metal roof stretches between two pavilions. The west pavilion, built from standing-seam Galvalume siding and aluminum sliding pocket doors, contains a changing room with translucent glass walls that provide light as well as privacy. Next to the changing room is a bath connected to an outdoor shower. The east pavilion uses metalized translucent glass, aluminum doors, and acrylic stucco to enclose a kitchen and connect an outdoor cooking area to the central covered exterior space. A poured-in-place concrete slab floor with lithochrome staining extends from the interior spaces to the outdoor areas. The stucco is gray to blend with the metal and the steel structure, a shade of red close to primed steel to express the material. The 16-foot-square (1.4-meter-square) eastern bay of the central space between the two pavilions has motorized insect screens that can be rolled down at night.

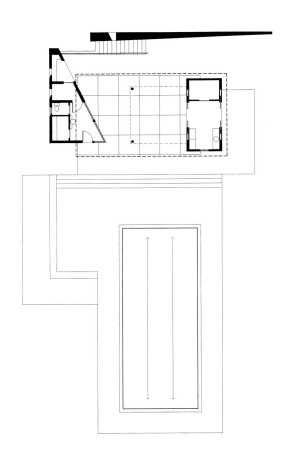

Above:
Site Plan

Right:
Looking north across the pool to the pool house and the wedge-shaped retaining wall and stair between the two pavilions.

Top left:
Looking south to the pool house from the path to the main house. A rectangular opening in the wedge-shaped retaining wall offers a glimpse of the pool. The outdoor shower area is beyond the aluminum louver door at the west pavilion.

Above left:
To increase the play of light and shade on the structure, the curved metal roof that stretches between the two pavilions engages the east pavilion and hovers above the west.

Top right:
At twilight, lights inside the west pavilion glow behind the translucent glass wall, and the metal roof reflects the overhead lighting.

Above right:
Detail of the exterior wall.

*At the base of the stairs a
shaded cloister provides a
transition from the outdoors
to the covered court.*

LAKE/FLATO

LISTENING TO THE WIND

Lake/Flato Architects use the lessons of old Texas ranch, farm, and industrial buildings to site and design houses that provide shade from the sun and catch every available breeze. Outdoor rooms—courtyards, screened porches, shaded walkways, dog-runs, and miradors (lookouts)—are as essential to the design of their buildings as the enclosed spaces.

The partners in the firm, Ted Flato and David Lake, both grew up in Texas. After receiving his degree in architecture from the University of Texas at Austin, Flato moved to the Panhandle where he built sodbuster farm buildings. "The farmers were amused at the notion of cows grazing on the roof," he recalls. Lake earned his architecture degree at Stanford, where he studied with William Turnbull, whose sensitivity to site and context is unsurpassed. Lake and Flato met while working for the San Antonio firm Ford Powell Carson, where they found a mentor in O'Neil Ford, who developed a form of vernacular modernism in Texas.

Since forming their own partnership in San Antonio, they have created buildings that have won numerous awards and, perhaps more importantly, provided their owners with lasting comfort and joy. William Turnbull wrote: "[Lake/Flato] make thoughtful buildings that consider space and light and the tough climate of their native southwest. They site buildings sensitively in an unforgiving Texas landscape and build them of elegantly crafted, commonplace materials. . . . Timeless architecture needn't shout; in south Texas it is more pleasant to listen to the wind whispering through it."

For one of their early projects, La Estrella Ranch, located 35 miles (56.5 kilometers) north of the Rio Grande River and 85 miles (137 kilometers) west of the Gulf of Mexico, Lake/Flato linked a compound of new and existing buildings with porches, breeze-ways, and tall walls that surround a courtyard in the style of a Mexican hacienda. The porches serve as open-air corridors and as outdoor rooms for dining and entertaining nine months of the year. The courtyard is a cool, fragrant oasis that provides the one-room deep surrounding interior spaces with cross-ventilation and the soothing sound of a fountain.

The Alamo Cement House was completed just a year later. For clients on a tight budget, Lake/Flato recycled parts of an abandoned 1920s steel-framed cement plant, and reassembled it on a ranch in the Texas Hill Country south of Austin. Outdoor rooms are intrinsic to the new design, which consists of three pavilions: a center building with a dog run in the middle that helps ventilate it; an open pavilion that defines the entry court and is used as a

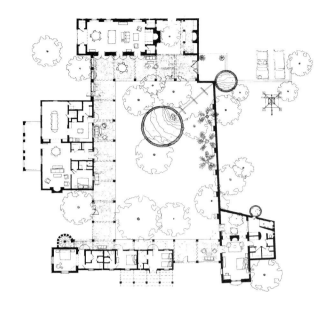

La Estrella Ranch
Site Plan

garage and machine shed; and the largest of the three, which is clad with insect screen to form a Texas-sized porch.

When a client with a parcel of land 60 feet (18.3 meters) above the Llano River in Central Texas asked for a house that would take advantage of the splendid views and connect strongly with the outdoors without disturbing the stark beauty of the bluffs, Lake/Flato designed a house with a long arching porch. The porch serves as the main entry to the house and an outdoor hallway that provides access to three independent bedrooms and baths and connects them to a large octagonal living room at the opposite end of the house.

Lake/Flato's design for a weekend retreat for a young family on the banks of Lake L.B.J. incorporates a variety of outdoor living rooms. They sited the house at the lakeside edge of the property, so it is cooled by breezes off the water, and the front lawn functions as a playing field for the children. Doors open the large octagonal living room to a porch overlooking the lake. A separate guest house above a boat house is reached by a bridge that leads to a dog run between the two guest rooms. The dog run is an outdoor living/dining room for the guest house. In the main house the kitchen connects a two-story living room to a large screened porch that has its own fireplace and kitchen, as well as dining and game tables. Leaves rustle and mosquitoes buzz outside the screens, but the wind whispers through.

New brick floors were extended to the existing porches, which were cleaned and painted.

The west end of the porch is enclosed by a wood screen that filters the harsh sunlight while maintaining cross-ventilation.

Alamo Cement Plant
Above:
Lake/Flato divided a steel shed from the Alamo Cement Plant into three parts: the center building, clad in galvanized metal, contains the master bedroom, library, and an open dog-run; the open structure on the left is used as a garage and machine shed; and a second-story guest room floats inside full-height screen walls.

Right:
Inside the screen porch the steel frame reaches up to 20 feet (6.1 meters) at the eaves. The porch provides a shady, protected place for outdoor dining.

Top:
In a corner of the porch a cube made of Texas limestone encloses a living room and kitchen, and provides a wall to cold winter winds. A salvaged cast-iron stair rises to a roof terrace and guest bedroom

Right:
The house is a collage of industrial materials: steel frame, corrugated metal, horizontal screen bands, native limestone walls, and recycled kiln brick.

Below:
Floor Plans

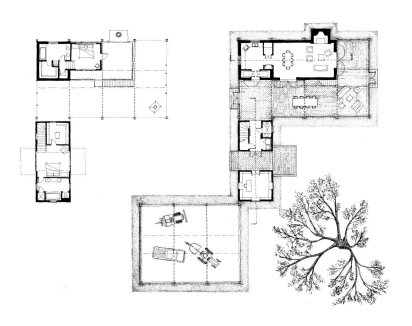

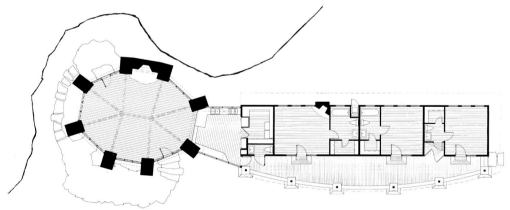

Chandler Ranch
Top:
The house sits solidly on a lime-
stone cliff 60 feet (18.3 meters)
above the Llano River in
Central Texas.

Above:
Floor Plan

Top:
The long arching porch provides access to the bedrooms
and extends their space to the
outdoors and the river view.

Above:
View from one of the bedrooms
to the porch.

The House on Lake L.B.J.
Top left:
The house, center, with the screen porch on the right and boat house on the left, are set at the end of a rounded peninsula that slopes down to the banks of Lake L.B.J. A circular field of grass ringed by trees is used as an open-air court.

Top right:
A view of the house from the lake.

Bottom:
Site Plan

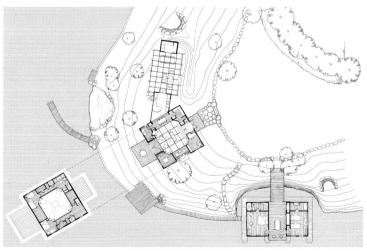

The living room extends out to a porch through French doors.

Following pages:
A hammock outside the screen porch is a shady place for relaxing.

Top left:
The porch is shaded by an exten-
sion of the roof and tall trees.

Above left:
A fireplace in the screen porch
provides campfire-like warmth
for cool winter nights. French
doors open to the kitchen,
which resembles a separate
house with its own pitched roof.

Top right:
The guest house breezeway
serves as a living/dining room
for the two guest rooms on
either side. Rolling barn doors
conceal a kitchenette.

Above right:
The screen porch with its
lakeside view is a favorite spot
for meals.

*The porch is set just above
the lake.*

CINI BOERI

EXTENDING LIFE TO THE OUTDOORS

Born and educated in Milan where she received a degree from the Politecnico, Cini Boeri worked with Marco Zanuso for over a decade before opening an independent studio in 1963. She says that at the time, "there were only a few women working in the field and specifically in my country, just two or three." Boeri believes being a woman excluded her from major commercial and institutional architectural commissions. Instead she worked on the design of apartments, houses, shops, showrooms, and offices. In the Italian tradition, her practice also encompasses furniture and industrial design. "In Italy," she explains, "the culture of design is inextricably linked with architecture and consequently I have simultaneously carried on both activities."

Boeri has devoted particular attention to the domestic realm, focusing, she says, "on the psychological relationship between man and his habitat." She considers the ability to enjoy nature essential to people's well-being. "Architecture is par excellence something human," she says, "and for its inhabitants it should offer warmth, the pleasure of feeling secure, simplicity and the joy of nature. . . . I try to leave the natural characteristics of the landscape outside without modifying them, just as if the house had fallen from the sky without disturbing nature." She sees outdoor living as a natural extension of the interior rooms in the houses she has designed, even when working in such challenging landscapes as the rocky Sardinian coast.

Several years after opening her studio, Boeri designed a house on the rocky cliffs of La Maddalena, an island off the coast of Sardinia. Although it is sited on the part of the island most exposed to the wind, perched on rocks that lead down to the sea,

an outdoor space is essential to the design. The living room and all four bedrooms have direct access to a central patio with cooking and living areas. The patio is sheltered from the wind by the double walls of the house connected by trapezoidal beams.

Her plan for a holiday house built in the same period on La Maddalena, for clients who requested that every room be equidistant to an open patio, arcs around a patio. Bedrooms, living, and dining rooms all have views facing the sea and direct access to the patio. The enclosing arc of the house protects the patio from the north wind that whips the Sardinian coast on blustery days.

Years later, designing a two-story villa in Porrentruy, Switzerland, amidst the fields and trees of the Alsatian countryside, Boeri created a patio protected by the sloping roof. Terraces are cut into the roof on the second story above the patio.

More recently, in the Italian hills near Pacenza, Boeri linked a cottage she restored to a new building with a second-floor glazed gallery. On the second floor the new portion has a large terrace that overlooks the valley. An outdoor dining platform is protected by a white Tendarch awning that shades the table and reflects the heat.

Describing her dream of an architecture for the future, Boeri writes, "I will see glass reflecting light, replacing rooftops, in which not only people but also the sky and the sea will be mirrored." Her dream for the future exists today in the outdoor rooms she has created.

House on the Cliffs
of La Maddalena
Top Right:
This house is perched on the
rocks on the windiest part of
the island of La Maddalena,
Sardinia.

Below:
The patio extends the living
room outside toward the sea.

**Holiday House on
La Maddalena**
*Top Left:
Concrete block walls are painted to blend with the sky and
sea. Narrow, slit-like windows
give the house the impression
of a fortress built into the rocky
landscape.*

*Bottom Left and Right:
Patio is used for outdoor dining.*

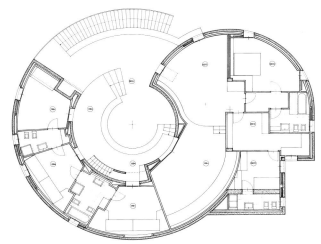

Top:
Floor Plan

Above:
View from above shows
how the house arcs around the
central patio.

Villa in Porrentruy, Switzerland
*Looking across the swimming
pool to the patio; the steeply
pitched roof is cut out over
a patio at ground level with
terraces above.*

Inside the patio showing the cutouts in the roof that slope to the ground.

Villa in Vigolzone
Top:
The original, remodeled brick house is joined to the new, wood house by a glazed gallery on the upper level.

Above:
A stone path leads to the dining platform under the white awning.

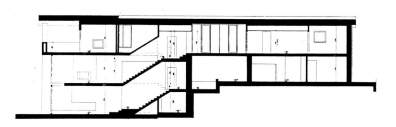

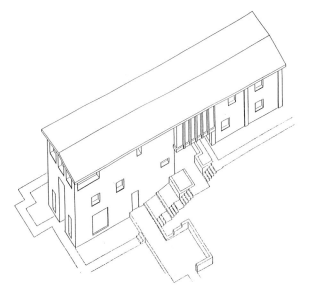

Top:
Section

Above:
Boeri designed the high and
narrow elevation of the new
house to recall farmhouse towers common to the countryside.
A terrace overlooks the valley.

Left:
Axonometric

STEVEN EHRLICH

OUT OF AFRICA

Living and working in Africa during the 1970s "opened my eyes and heart to the concept of outdoor living," Steven Ehrlich says. While serving in the Peace Corps, Ehrlich was assigned to the Moroccan Architecture and Planning office in Marrakesh. Later he traveled in and around North and West Africa's Sahara desert. During his last three years in Africa he taught architecture at Ahmadu Bello University in Zaria, Nigeria.

Although born in York City and raised and educated in the east, when Ehrlich returned to the United States in 1976, he was attracted to Southern California, believing that the freedom from architectural tradition there offered young architects an opportunity to do innovative work. Moreover, the climate was conducive to the design of the outdoor rooms he had come to admire while living in Africa. Although he continues to have an abiding respect for the aesthetics of other cultures, he considers himself a modernist, and finds that the simplicity of vernacular forms and the relationship between form and function in the design of African housing is in harmony with modernism.

The house in Santa Monica that Ehrlich designed for his own family in 1988 exemplifies his belief in the relevance of the courtyard, for both urban and suburban living, to reinforce our connection to nature "by editing out environmental pollution." A canyon wall at the back of his property encloses a terraced courtyard visible to the three-story house through a wall of glass. The canyon wall shields the house from the city, while the upper levels of the house offer views of the ocean. Ehrlich has provided his family with a variety of rooms for outdoor living: "Three terraces carved from the hillside form the multi-level courtyard cool with fern and flower. Each story has its own corresponding garden terrace, the upper two reached via bridges leading from the second and third floor," he explains. With time the planted materials grow increasingly lush, covering the built structure so that the outdoors spaces seem to be sculpted from the landscape.

With the Gold-Friedman residence, a house designed by Ehrlich several years later in the same neighborhood as his own, he extended his ideas of a hillside courtyard house. Here too, the space between the house and the canyon wall is a multi-level garden court. A patio with built-in seating, pool, and fountain are constructed with colorful Italian tiles, and a bridge connects the house to the terraced hillside. More outdoor spaces form an entry sequence on the street side of the house, where a multi-platformed stairway leads to a broad front porch.

Steven Ehrlich Architects, the firm he founded in 1979, is involved in a variety of commissions including civic and commercial projects, as well as the continued design of residences and the exploration of the effect of new materials and technology on the design of outdoor rooms. "The outdoor spaces I design are always engaged in vociferous dialogue with adjacent indoor spaces," he says. "Through technology of new materials and mechanical systems, glass walls can slide away, thus evaporating the barrier between the two."

An addition Ehrlich designed for a beach house by Richard Neutra in Santa Monica is a stunning example of his use of new materials and technology to dissolve the barrier between interior and outdoor rooms. The present owners wanted to restore the original house and requested additional garages, servant's quarters, and entertaining space. Ehrlich believed that it was important to relate to the Neutra house without mimicking it. He meticulously restored the original building inside and out. The owner's acquisition of an adjacent lot made it possible for him to build an L-shaped wing at the front of the property that encompasses additional garage space with a servant's apartment above. The street-side structure provides a barrier from the noise of the Pacific Coast Highway and encloses a courtyard that provides space for a dramatic steel and glass entertaining pavilion that serves the family as a media center, entertaining room, and poolside cabana. It is linked to the original house by a glass bridge, and it has access to a new pool designed by Barry Beer, who also did the landscape design. The steel gate at the end of the pool opens with the press of a button to reveal the ocean view. Three of the pavilion's walls are glass, and the glass at the east and west ends slides into a pocket between two concrete walls, transforming the enclosed room into an airy, shaded outdoor space. Even with this exercise in contemporary technology, Ehrlich continues to respect the lessons he learned in Africa. "A courtyard helps a house become a retreat," he says. "I was giving a primitive idea a modern voice."

Ehrlich Residence
Right:
Front doors open to a pocket courtyard. Stairs inside and out rise to the main level.

Top left:
A Japanese maple, jasmine, and bamboo transform the small front court into a lush oasis.

Above left:
View of the dining deck with door open to the kitchen. "Rosemary can be plucked to enhance meals cooked on a barbecue that can be rolled outdoors," Ehrlich says.

Top right:
Wisteria cascades from the bridge that forms a trellis above a deck for outdoor dining adjacent to the kitchen.

Above right:
The outdoor wood furniture designed by Ehrlich was inspired by Reitveld.

Right:
The architect's three-story house connects to the outdoors on every level. A bridge leads from the top floor of the house to the hills.

Gold-Friedman Residence
Below left:
A series of small landscaped areas enhance the path up to the entrance of the house, a story above the street.

Bottom:
Doors open the house to an outdoor patio highlighted with colorful Italian tile. A "truss-bridge" connects the house to the hillside.

Below right:
The perimeter of the patio is defined by a retaining wall with built-in seating and pool.

Water spills from a fountain in front of a copper plate. The shimmering water increases the vibrancy of the colors.

Addition to Neutra Beach House
Top:
The curved roof of the pavilion is Ehrlich's response to the bay window facing the ocean in the Neutra house. Glass doors at the east and west ends of the pavilion slide open. A glass-enclosed corridor links the addition to the house.

Below:
Inside the pavilion, wood doors conceal a media center. The perforated stainless steel ceiling absorbs sound. Acid washed concrete floors extend out to the pool deck.

Top:
View down from the main
house to the pavilion, which
appears to float within the
courtyard. The roof is standing-
seam brushed stainless steel.

Below:
Sketches

Following pages:
Looking across the new swimming pool, a bluff capped by
palm trees forms a dramatic
backdrop for the pavilion. An
alcove on the right encloses a
barbecue. The 1940s double
lounge chair was designed by
Walter Lamb.

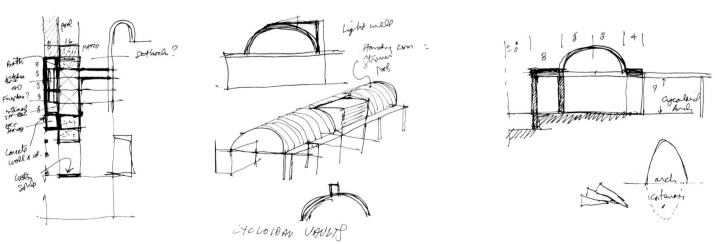

Below left:
Steel gates at the end of the pool
open to reveal the Pacific Ocean.

Below right:
The stainless steel gate closed.
Ehrlich describes it as "kinetic art."

Right:
The steel structural system is,
Ehrlich says, "a reinterpreted
quote" from the spider leg
supports Neutra used in some
of his later houses.

CENTERBROOK

INSTILLING THE LANDSCAPE WITH INTIMACY

As Charles Moore moved about the country from one academic post to another, students joined him in his quest to bring a sense of place, history, and humor back to architecture. Centerbrook is one of several architectural firms that grew from these alliances and carries on his legacy of creating buildings that celebrate vernacular architecture and the land on which they are built. Moore established the firm in New Haven when he moved east from Berkeley, California to become chairman of Yale's department of architecture. In 1970 he moved the office 25 miles (16 kilometers) from New Haven to Centerbrook, a village that is now part of the town of Essex, Connecticut, where he had bought an abandoned nineteenth-century factory building and transformed it into architectural studios. The offices have since been expanded with new buildings that reflect the character of the originals.

Now renamed for the town of Centerbrook, the firm has been described as five practices under one roof, with each of the five partners—Mark Simon, William H. Grover, Jefferson B. Riley, Chad Floyd, and James C. Childress—responsible for his own marketing, business, and production. The partners continue to share the values of their founder, Charles Moore, including his keen interest in gardens. Chad Floyd credits landscape architect Lester Collins for refining the firm's focus on the relationship of projects with the outdoor world during the decade that the partners collaborated with him. "What we found ourselves trying to create then with Lester—and what we carry on making today without him—are outdoor rooms, plain and simple, rooms that lead in engaging sequences from the macro-scale of the landscape at large to the intimacy of small backyard terraces, and from there seamlessly, we hope, to interesting rooms within," Floyd says.

In designing a house on the Connecticut shore with a southerly view of the Long Island Sound, a rocky island to the southeast, and the Thimble Islands to the southwest, Floyd enhanced the residents' enjoyment of the spectacular site by creating a series of decks and terraces that serve as outdoor rooms and open-air corridors.

The partners often use native materials to integrate outdoor spaces into the landscape. For example, Mark Simon used local pink granite to create site walls and steps that on the sea side outline a plunge pool for a house he designed on a rocky outcropping on the Connecticut coast between the Long Island Sound and a bird-inhabited marsh surrounding abandoned granite quarries.

When called on to design additions to existing houses, Centerbrook aspires never to overwhelm either the landscape or existing buildings. Jefferson Riley concealed a large addition to a nineteenth-century farmhouse in New York State's Hudson

Valley in what appears from the road to be a string of traditional barns. He moved the guest entrance from the front door of the old house to a new entry court/herb garden from which one can proceed into the old house or under a covered passage to the new facilities, each of which has a special connection to the outdoors. The back gardens and terraces look out over the pool to a pond and the woods.

Charged with renovating and adding on to an existing contemporary house built in the 1970s in southern Connecticut, William Grover added a gable roof to the flat-roofed garage, a new bedroom wing, and pool house. He organized these buildings into a small "village" surrounding a forecourt that replaced a circular driveway.

Working with landscape architect Lester Collins, Jim Childress created a garden for a neo-Gothic house that had once been the center of a large estate and is now surrounded by an urban area. The garden provides the owners with an escape from the city while also enhancing the neighborhood. A terraced path connects several gardens. The path leads to a grand porch that overlooks a large lawn that is shared with the neighborhood.

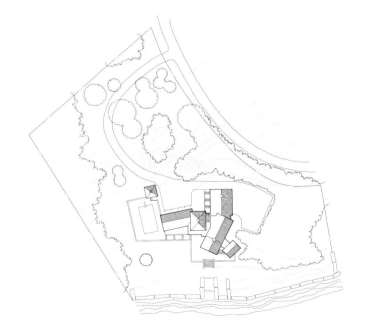

House on the Connecticut Shore
Above:
Site Plan

Right:
A pool forms the largest
outdoor room.

Top:
The deck climbs up between the
pavilions of the house with
steps that remind its architect of
a hill town.

Above:
The deck surrounding the house
provides outdoor spaces of
varying privacy.

Right:
The latticed deck surrounding
the house forms a base on
which its architect designed "a
village of pavilions."

House in Southern Connecticut
Top left:
Charged with renovating and adding on to a 1970s house, Bill Grover used three different colors to "make it seem more like a village than a villa."

Left:
A steel-framed deck surrounds a tree. The thin steel rod used to construct the railing was painted black to make it as unobtrusive as possible.

Top right:
Walls surrounding the pool are made of Stoney Creek pink granite. The railing and gate are bronze.

Above:
Wood stairs curve up to the deck where a bench is built in around the tree trunk.

Urban Garden
Top:
A terraced path connects the gardens created around this Gothic-style house. Walls with cascading flowering plants line the path that leads to the front lawn past an outdoor room that is partially shaded by a magnolia tree.

Above left:
A new trellis planted with clematis echoes the Gothic style of the house into the garden.

Above right:
A garden carpeted with perennials is surrounded by yews.

Right:
A fountain made from a grist wheel found on the site masks noise from the surrounding city.

WALTER CHATHAM
LOFTY GARDENS

Whether designing on the islands of Nevis or Manhattan, Walter Chatham always looks to the local architecture to see what works well. He does the same with gardens, and whether the residences are on a Caribbean Island, Florida, Mississippi, or New York City, where he lives and heads his own architectural firm, Chatham always incorporates outdoor rooms into his designs. Although he compares the climate of New York City to Mars, with its extreme temperatures and red skies, he has created roof gardens for both his family's lofts in Manhattan's downtown Soho neighborhood. He applied the same guiding principles he uses for outdoor rooms in the country: to create a sense of enclosure but still feel that you are outdoors you need walls on at least one side, preferably two or three, but never all four, and small structures to magnify the scale of the plants and vistas.

The Chatham's first Soho loft occupied the two top floors of one of the tallest buildings in the vacinity. The roof was enclosed by the building's slanting cornice on the north and east sides and by a parapet on the south end. He built a deck that spans the length of the roof and raised it so the family and their guests could enjoy the view of the Manhattan skyline over the south wall. The raised deck also made it possible to put in a Japanese reflecting pool just outside the entrance. A corrugated aluminum tool shed sparkles under the sun like a small, shiny tent—a modernist folly in the urban garden. "The deck furniture," he says, "was catch as catch can"—some left from the former owner, some from Wave Hill. Confining the garden to pots gives flexibility for rearrangement.

When the Chathams moved into their second loft in a building that was an abandoned power plant, the roof had no insulation, so once again they built a deck. When renovating a space Chatham generates the design from what remains, using both the physical and historical facts. Here, he installed an orange steel staircase, a reminder of the power plant that had been there before, to lead up to his wife's studio and out to the deck. The roof garden is punctuated by four raised skylights that provide focal points on the endless horizon of sky that extends over the rooftops. He says they give the deck the feel of being on an aircraft carrier. It took fourteen years of growing time and experimentation for the plants on their first roof garden to become lush. Herbs and anything resembling a weed seemed to flourish, as well as plants with hardy roots dug up on his father-in-law's West Virginia property. Given time, nature finds her way, even in Manhattan. Recently a zinnia appeared uninvited, a gift from a passing bird flying over the rooftops.

First Chatham Loft
Top:
View of downtown Manhattan includes the World Trade Towers. A glass dome protects books from changes in the weather.

Above:
At night the glow of lights from the children's apartment, which occupied the top floor of the loft, is reflected in the Japanese pool.

The raised deck made it possible to put in a Japanese reflecting pool above the roof drain just outside the entrance.

Top:
Floor Plan

Above:
The roof garden served as a
playground for the children
with a sandbox and sprinkler.

Right:
Caribbean buildings provided
the inspiration for the corrugated aluminum tool shed.

Second Chatham Loft
Left:
An open door leads from Mary Adams Chatham's rooftop studio to the family's new roof garden.

Top:
Dining table and chairs are just outside the door to the roof where once again the Chathams are growing an herb and flower garden in containers. On left, one of the skylights.

Below:
Floor Plan

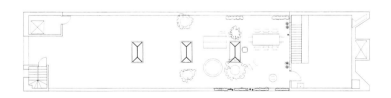

Below:
The three Chatham children
enjoy a rooftop playground
created from Rubbermaid toys.

Right:
In the evening lights from
the downtown towers provide
a glittering backdrop for outdoor dining.

ALBERTO CAMPO BAEZA
REFLECTING LIGHT

A native of Spain, Alberto Campo Baeza has combined a teaching career with a thriving architectural practice. In 1986, just four years after earning his Ph.D. in architecture from the ETSAM University in Madrid, he became the chairman of design for the university. The firm he heads in Madrid has produced numerous educational and public buildings, and a series of small pristine houses that recall the purity of Le Corbusier's villas.

In Campo Baeza's houses materials flow seamlessly between the indoor and outdoor spaces, usually separated only by frameless windows placed to receive light reflected off the white walls surrounding the courtyards and terraces. Stucco walls, inside and out, enclose his rooms. Light, frequently directed in diagonal shafts, infuses the spaces with the transfiguring reflections seen in Vermeer's paintings. The houses he designs are at once mysterious and serene.

Campo Baeza calls the Turegano house, one of his earliest projects, "a white and cubic hut." To comply with the building codes of the small hillside site in Pozuelo, Madrid, the house measures only 33 by 33 by 33 feet (10.1 by 10.1 by 10.1 meters). The simple "hut" is transformed by light, as it makes its journey from east to southwest, captured through windows facing a garden and terraces.

On a corner lot, measuring 50 by 69 feet (15.2 by 21.0 meters), on the outskirts of a traditional suburb of Madrid, Campo Baeza designed a house that is a box within a box. Outdoor rooms are tightly woven into the plan. White stucco walls surround the property forming the outer box of the Garcia Marcos house. A pool is carved into the patio on one side. High walls enclose a rooftop terrace to form an open-air room. "Through light and proportion, a small and simple closed house is converted into a grand and open one, where, with almost nothing, everything is possible. It is a miracle box," he says.

In the early 1990s Campo Baeza was asked to design secure housing for the personnel of the Spanish Embassy in Algiers. The residences occupy a sloping site in the garden of the ambassador's residence. Campo Baeza says his proposal was for "four white boxes to be planted among palm trees and with walls forming patios and terraces." He placed the living rooms on the ground floors adjacent to walled courtyards. Rooftop terraces offer views of the Bay of Algiers.

Campo Baeza designed the Casa Gaspar on flat land in the middle of an orange grove for a family that asked for total privacy. He enclosed the entire compound with a surrounding wall nearly ten feet high (3 meters) with only a pedestrian and garage door open to the outside. The interior rooms of the house are arranged in a strip in the center allowing the remaining two-thirds of the compound to be outdoor rooms. The living room has a large patio on either side, each one planted with two orange trees. The bedrooms and kitchen have their own separate outdoor rooms. Campo Baeza writes about the outdoor rooms of the Casa Gaspar describing an artist arriving at the orange grove and deciding to establish a resting place there:

> *He planted four green lemon trees, two in the patio in front, and the other two in the patio behind. And there, in the back, ending the axis of all the doors, he dug a grave from the earth from where the water came to sing, waking up lemon trees in white lemon blossoms which flooded the air with the scent of paradise. And the artist thought that this space of the PRESENT ABSENCE full of light and silence and beauty, was preferable to the medley outside in which our society was wracking. And seeing that that which he had made was good, he rested there to live happily ever after.*

Turegano House
Top left:
Model demonstrates how the rooms, inside and out, are arranged on the hillside property.

Below left:
Section sketch

Above left:
A wall along the street side of the house provides privacy and enclosed outdoor rooms.

Above right:
Large windows face the garden on the south side.

Right:
Axonometric

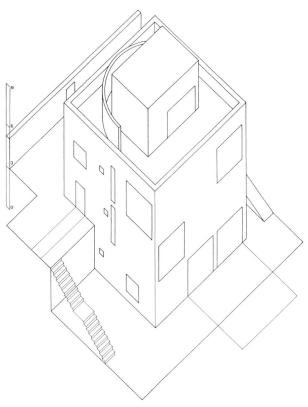

Garcia Marcos House

Top:
The house occupies a corner site in a conventional suburb of Madrid.

Below left:
East-west section of the model shows how the space flows out to the patio at ground level and to the sky room on top of the house.

Below right:
Axonometric

Right:
Glass doors open the house to the patio next to the pool.

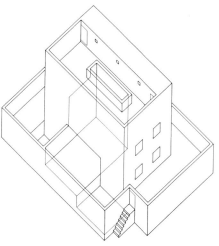

Four Villas in Algiers
Top:
The street-sides of the villas are
very private. Rooftop terraces
offer a view of the Algerian bay.

Below:
The villas are entered at the inter-
mediary level from the stree.

*The living rooms placed at garden
level open to walled courtyards.*

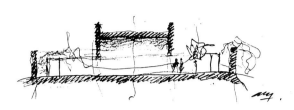

Gaspar House
Top left:
The entrance patio.

Top right:
Section sketch

Above:
Section of the model demon-
strates how Campo Baeza
divided the compound into
three parts, leaving all but the
center portion open to the sky.

Above:
In response to the client's
request for absolute privacy,
Campo Baeza designed a
"closed grove" behind a 12-
foot (3.7-meter) wall.

*Water in a pool in the back
courtyard of the house, according to Baeza, "came to sing,
waking up lemon trees in white
lemon blossoms which flood the
air with the scent of Paradise."*

Below:
The continuity of space from
inside and out is emphasized by
the use of the same materials, the
white stucco walls and limestone
floors, kept at the same grade

Right:
Interior rooms flow seamlessly to
adjacent patios through large
frameless doors.

MOORE RUBLE YUDELL

DWELLING IN THE LANDSCAPE

"In our design of porches, courtyards, and pergolas, we seek to provide a special sense of habitation in which we experience the primal feeling of protection while we absorb and appreciate the outside realm," says Buzz Yudell, a partner in the Santa Monica-based firm Moore Ruble Yudell. MRY is one of several collaborative firms established by Charles Moore as he moved across the country from one academic post to another. In 1976, Yudell and his wife Tina Beebe, a color consultant and landscape designer, answered the call of their mentor, Charles Moore to move from the east to Southern California where Yudell became a partner in Moore's new firm.

The couple began searching for land near the ocean, where they could build a courtyard house that would enable them to live more intimately in the landscape. After years of searching, the only affordable lot they found was on a Malibu hillside, bordered on one side by a dry river bed and on the other by a neighbor's stables. The buildable portion of the lot was only 600 feet (183-meters) long by 32 feet (9.8 meters) wide. While other buyers could not imagine what to do with such an oddly shaped piece of land, Yudell and Beebe were intrigued by the property that slopes from a view of the mountains to the north toward a view southward of the Pacific Ocean.

Their design evolved from the constraints of the site setbacks that dictated that the house be long and skinny. The property would not accommodate a house shaped around a courtyard. Instead, a long gallery runs along one side of the main rooms of the house: a kitchen/sitting room and a living/dining room. French doors

open the gallery to a paved street that steps down the slope past a series of garden rooms—pergolas, trellises, and a rose court. On the lowest level a blue lap pool stretches toward the distant view of the ocean. On the second floor the master bedroom opens to a sleeping porch with a view of the Pacific.

The plan allows for enormous flexibility. Meals are often taken in one of the many outdoor rooms. Parties flow over from the gallery to the terraces and down to a canvas-covered pool pavilion. Breezes scented with lavender, eucalyptus, and lemon verbena bring the outdoors inside. On land that was once a tomato field, Beebe, an accomplished gardener, grows fruits and vegetables as well as flowers. She and Yudell may begin the day with breakfast served under one of the pergolas laden with climbing roses. Their glasses are filled with crimson-colored juice squeezed from blood oranges picked from their own trees. Lunch is sometimes served poolside under the striped pavilion; dinner guests may enjoy food prepared on the outdoor grill and served under a vine-covered pergola.

"The longer we practice architecture, the more we feel that buildings should live in and of the landscape," Yudell says. This awareness, increased by the experiences their own house provides, has resulted in the design of buildings in which the spaces between or on the edge are shaped as thoughtfully as the enclosed rooms. These outdoor rooms are planned to provide a range from bright through dappled light to dusk and darkness.

Recently, MRY designed a house for a family in Pacific Palisades where, Yudell says, "the character comes from the shaping of courtyards between building elements." Inspired by a convent in Patzcuaro, Mexico, known as *once patios* (eleven patios), MRY decided to try for twelve. The house evolved into an H-shaped plan in which all major rooms merge with gardens and courts of diverse character that complement the interior spaces. The library, for example, opens to a small "secret" garden that Yudell says is "a contemplative complement to its interior partner. . . . As a whole the house and garden seek to provide the family with a place at once intimate and grand, full of choice and surprise yet rooted to its landscape."

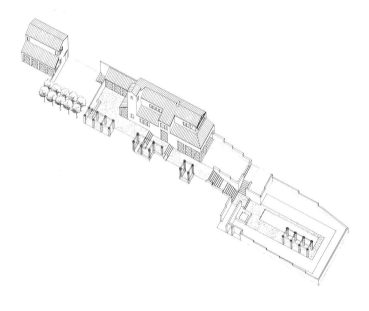

Yudell/Beebe House
Left:
Axonometric

Right:
French doors open to the gardens from a gallery that runs the length of the house.

Top:
Near the lap pool Percy Yudell
is joined by his friend Honey.

Below:
Outdoor rooms are linked by
a terraced pathway that steps
down to the pool

Top:
In an outdoor room at one end
of the gardens a canvas-covered
banquette provides another
pleasant spot for relaxation.

Below:
Inside the poolside pavilion
comfortable wicker armchairs
surround a table.

Above:
Inside the pergola-framed gardens, lush with blooms, looking toward a hammock.

Right:
The entrance court.

House in the Pacific Palisades
Top:
Seen from the Olive grove, a series of outdoor rooms step down from left to right: the loggia, Jacaranda grove, rose garden, overlook, living room terrace, lap pool and lower pool terrace.

Below:
Site Plan

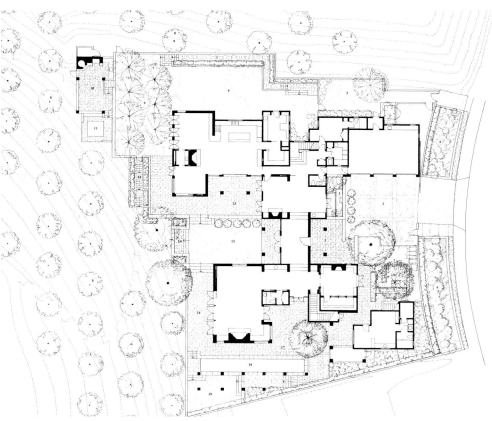

Below:
French doors open the living room to a terrace. Steps lead up to a formal lawn bordered by the dining room entrance.

Bottom:
The loggia overlooks the Olive grove and the mountains beyond.

Following pages:
View west of the trellis, lap pool and, on the right, the living room terrace.

RICARDO LEGORRETA
ROOMS FOR THE SPIRIT

Ricardo Legorreta's architecture is so closely integrated with nature that he seems to use the earth and sky as building materials. In his buildings, both in his native Mexico and in the United States, there are rooms where the sky is the ceiling and the floor, a pool of sparkling water. Windows are often left as open apertures in walls designed to emit light in a particular way. He writes, "Earth and sky, light and color, walls and plaster, essence of beauty, spirituality, and life."

In 1964 at the dedication of his first major building, a Chrysler factory in Tasluca, Mexico, Legorreta had a seminal meeting with the legendary Mexican architect, Luis Barragan. When he asked Barragan to comment on the building, Barragan said, "You need to pay more attention to landscaping; it is an integral part of architecture." Several years after his meeting with Barragan, they collaborated on the landscaping of the Camino Real Mexico Hotel where Legorreta had designed a large central courtyard as well as smaller patios for clusters of guest rooms. In the Hispanic tradition, they incorporated water into the outdoor spaces. Since then, whether designing another hotel, a factory, an office building, or a museum, he always integrates outdoor spaces into his designs. In his houses, courtyards, terraces, patios, and enclosed gardens invite the inhabitants to enjoy the outdoors as part of their daily lives.

Legorreta's work has been significantly influenced by Mexico's vernacular architecture: the simplicity of pre-Colombian architecture, the emotional quality of the colorful village houses. In Mexican architecture the wall is supremely important. Legorreta writes that it is the "essence of our architecture . . . limit of property and dreams." He did his first project outside his native country in 1985, when the Mexican actor Ricardo Montalban asked him to design a house in California's Hollywood Hills that would "represent Mexico in the modern sense." To give the family spectacular views of Los Angeles from the back of their site on a bluff while still preserving their privacy, Legorreta designed outdoor spaces behind the high, solid walls of the Mexican hacienda, and in the back a main terrace open to a view of the city.

Another California house Legoretta designed around the same time is on an expansive site overlooking the Santa Fe Valley, with no close neighbors. Large windows integrate the interiors with a variety of terraces, courtyards, and gardens. A gallery connects the main house to a guest house. Walls extend out from the house to partially enclose a pool, forming a room with an aquamarine carpet.

In a house called La Colorada, which Legorreta completed in Mexico's Valle de Bravo in 1996, outdoor and indoor rooms blend harmoniously, each enhancing the other. The entry is through a lemon orchard that ends in a circular motor court. Stairs lead up to the entrance past a fountain. Inside, every room opens to a patio or terrace. A sliding ceiling over the pool opens to the sky and closes to provide shade and intimacy.

The Casa Cervantes, completed the same year as La Colorada, stands on an irregular lot in Mexico City with close neighbors. Here privacy is provided with outdoor walls that extend from the house to enclose the patio and courtyard; even in a city house Legorreta designs to invite the inhabitants to enjoy the outdoors while working, resting, and eating. "If architecture doesn't contribute to human peace and happiness," he writes, "it deserves to disappear. A space can be beautiful, but if it doesn't raise your spirits, it is not architecture."

Montalban House
The house steps up a hill.

The front entrance to the house. Privacy is preserved by tall walls broken only by the front door and two small windows.

Below:
A spacious terrace at the back of the house is open to the views of Los Angeles.

Bottom left:
Floor tiles, terrace furniture, and many of the plants were brought from Mexico.

Bottom right:
Floor Plan

Right:
A lap pool with a fountain is placed at the edge of the terrace. Brightly colored walls enhance the spirit of the out-door room.

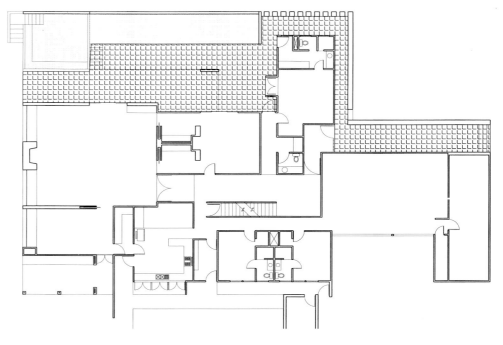

Rancho Santa Fe House

Top left:
The exterior of the library, where a tall chimney projects from the façade.

Below left:
The pool, bordered by a carpet of green grass, extends beyond the walls of the house.

Bottom:
Floor Plan

Top right:
Pastel colors enhance the playful atmosphere of the partially enclosed pool.

Below right:
Steps leading to the guest house. The same color was used on the walls and steps to create the sensation of not knowing where one ends and the other begins.

Facing page:
The latticed ceiling over the pool projects an ever-changing play of light.

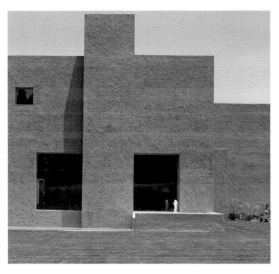

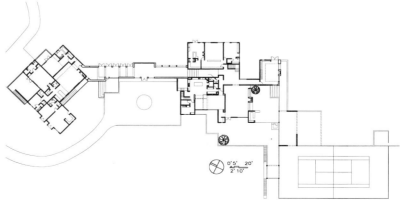

La Colorada

Below left:
A circular motor court at the entrance of the house with stone excavated and installed by local craftsmen.

Middle left:
The terrace off the living room with a view over the Valle de Bravo.

Bottom left:
Floor Plan

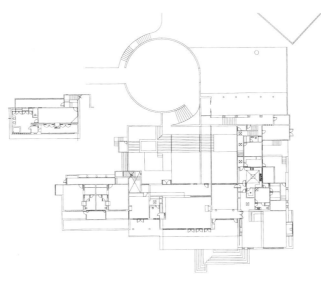

*Steps lead down from the motor
court to this courtyard with a
stone fountain.*

Below:
A stone dining table extends from
an opening in a cherry-red wall.

Right:
The latticed ceiling above
the pool may be opened to
the sky; closed, it projects an
ever-changing play of light
over the pool.

House in Mexico City
Facing page:
A tall wall in the patio provides privacy from neighboring houses.

Bottom left:
Section Drawing

Bottom right:
Floor Plan

Below left:
The breakfast room opens to a small patio where the owners enjoy reading the morning paper.

Below middle:
The fountain in the entry courtyard, where water spills onto a stone floor designed by the Mexican artist Vicente Rojo. The fountain is visible from the entrance, living room, and the breakfast patio.

Below right:
Another view of the fountain showing reflections of the brightly colored walls in the water.

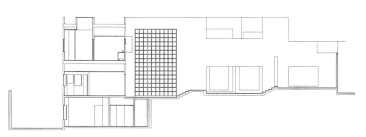

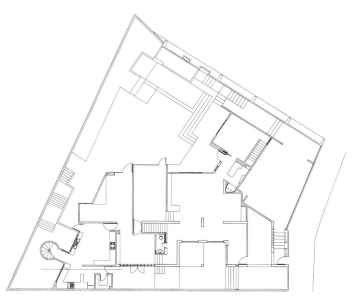

DIRECTORY OF ARCHITECTS

Tadao Ando Architect & Associates
5-23 Toyosaki
2 Chome
Kita-Ku
Osaka, Japan 531
Tel: 81-6-375-1148
Fax: 81-6-374-6240

Batter Kay Associates
110 15th Street
Del Mar, CA 92014
Tel: 619 755-1711
Fax: 619 481-3816

Cini Boeri
Studio archutettara dott. arch. Cini Boeri
Via Giovannino De Grassi, 4
20123 Milano
Italy
Tel: 02 875038-876301
Fax: 02 875531

Alberto Campo Baeza
Arquitecto
Almirante, 9
28004 Madrid
Spain
Tel/Fax: 34-1-521-7061

Centerbrook
Architects and Planners, LLC
Box 955
Essex, CT 06426
Tel: 860 767-0175
Fax: 860 767-8719

Walter Chatham
Architect
580 Broadway
New York, NY 10012
Tel: 212 925-2202
Fax: 212 966-2857

Charles Correa
Architects/Planners
9 Mathew Road
Bombay 400 004 India
Tel: 363-3307 and 364-5195
Fax: 91 (22) 363-1138

James Cutler
135 Parfitt Way SW
Bainbridge Island, WA 98110
Tel: 206 842-4710
Fax: 206 842-4420

Demetriades & Walker
10 Leonard Street
New York, NY 10013
Tel: 212 966-8807
Fax: 212 966-8834

Steven Ehrlich
Architect
10950 Washington Blvd., Suite 117
Culver City, CA 90232
Tel: 310 838-9700
Fax: 310 838-9737

Hugh Newell Jacobsen, F.A.I.A.
Architect
2529 P Street NW
Washington, DC 20007-3024
Tel: 202 337-5200
Fax: 337-3609

Susan Jennings
400 4th Street
Brooklyn, NY 11215
Tel: 718 788-3221

Lake/Flato Architects, Inc.
311 Third Street, Suite 200
San Antonio, TX 75205
Tel: 210 227-3335
Fax: 210 224-9515

Ricardo Legorreta Arquitectos
Palacio de Versalles #285-A
Mexico DF 11020
Mexico
Tel: 251 96 98
Fax: 506 61 62

Max Levy
Architect
5646 Milton Street
Suite 709
Dallas, TX 75206
Tel: 214 368-2023
Tel: 214 361-5467

Peter McMahon
504 Warren Street #1
Brooklyn, NY 11217
Tel: 718 797-0503

Moore Ruble Yudell
Architects
& Planners
933 Pico Boulevard
Santa Monica, CA 90405
Tel: 310 450-1400
Fax: 310 450-1403

Antoine Predock
Architect
300 12th Street NW
Albuquerque, New Mexico 87102
Tel: 505 842-7390
Tel: 505 243-6254

William Turnbull (Deceased)
Turnbull Griffin & Haesloop
Architects
Pier 1 1/2
The Embarcadero
San Francisco, CA 94111
Tel: 415 986-3642
Fax: 415 986-4778

PHOTO CREDITS

Cover
Sky House by Max Levy, photo by Scott Frances, courtesy of *House Beautiful*

Back cover
top: Walter Chatham loft, photo by Kari Haavisto, courtesy of *House Beautiful*; bottom: La Colorada house by Ricardo Legorreta, photo by Lourdes Legorreta.

Foreword
Blackmon Winter: page 8; A. Piovano and P. Albornoz: page 9 (left); Timothy Hursley: page 9 (right).

pages 12-13
Top row, left to right: Mary F. Nichols; Kari Haavisto, courtesy of *House Beautiful*; Paul Hester, courtesy of Lake/Flato; Ron Parello; Scott Frances, courtesy of *House Beautiful*; Timothy Hursley.
Second row: Lourdes Legorreta; Scott Frances, courtesy of *House Beautiful*; Kari Haavisto, courtesy of *House Beautiful*; Timothy Hursley.
Third row: Mitsuo Matsuoka; Francesco Radino; Francesco Radino; Timothy Hursley; Scott Frances, courtesy of *House Beautiful*; Robert Lautman, courtesy of *House Beautiful*.
Bottom row: Tim Street-Porter; Ron Parello; Lourdes Legorreta; Robert Lautman; Timothy Hursley, courtesy of *House Beautiful*; Mick Hales.

William Turnbull, In Case of Rain, *pages 14–19*
Mark Darley, courtesy of *House Beautiful*: all photos.

Charles Correa, Bestowing the Blessings of the Sky, *pages 20-31*
Claire Arni: pages 21–23, 26 (upper right, lower left); 27 (below); Charles Correa: pages 24–25, 26 (upper left, lower right); 27 (above), 29, 31; Rohinton Irani: page 28 (below).

James Cutler, Revering the Land, *pages 32–35*
Timothy Hursley, courtesy of *House Beautiful*: all photos.

Hugh Newell Jacobsen, Outdoor Reflections, *pages 36–49*
Robert Lautman: all photos.
Photos of House in Windsor, Florida (pages 44–45), and House in Athens, Greece (pages 48–49), courtesy of *House Beautiful*.

Max Levy, The Promise of Shade, *pages 50–55*
Scott Frances, courtesy of *House Beautiful*: all photos.

Tadao Ando, Abstracting Nature, *pages 56–63*
Mitsuo Matsuoka: all photos.

Antoine Predock, Icons in the Landscape, *pages 64–77*
Timothy Hursley: all photos.

Peter McMahon and Susan Jennings, Serving Nature, *pages 78–83*
Peter Aaron/ESTO, courtesy of *House Beautiful*: all photos.

Batter Kay Associates, Transparent Rooms, *pages 84–93*
Ron Parello: pages 84–89;
Jeremy Samuelson, courtesy of *House Beautiful*: pages 90–93.

Elizabeth Demetriades, A Foreground for Nature, *pages 94–97*
Michael Vitti: pages 95, 96 (upper row; lower row, left), 97; Patrick Walker: page 96 (lower row, right).

Lake/Flato, Listening to the Wind, *pages 98–111*
Blackmon Winter: page 99;
Paul Hester: pages 100–103; Timothy Hursley, courtesy of *House Beautiful*: pages 104–111.

Cini Boeri, Extending Life to the Outdoors, *pages 112–119*
Alberto Pinto: pages 112–113; Jacopo Faggioni: pages 114–115; Gabriele Basilico: pages 116–117; Francesco Radino: pages 118–119.

Steven Ehrlich, Out of Africa, *pages 120–131*
Tim Street–Porter: all photos.
Photos of Addition to Neutra Beach House (pages 126–131), courtesy of *House Beautiful*.

Centerbrook, Instilling the Landscape with Intimacy, *pages 132–143*
Mick Hales: pages 133–135; Jeff Goldberg/ESTO: pages 136–137, 140–143; Peter Aaron/ESTO: pages 138–139.

Walter Chatham, Lofty Gardens, *pages 144–151*
Kari Haavisto, courtesy of *House Beautiful*: pages 144–147; Scott Frances, courtesy of *House Beautiful*: pages 148–151.

Alberto Campo Baeza, Reflecting Light, *pages 152–163*
Hisao Suzuki: pages 152–153, 158–163; A. Piovano and P. Albornoz: pages 154–155; Colette Jauze: pages 156–157.

Moore Ruble Yudell, Dwelling in the Landscape, *pages 164–173*
John Vaughan, courtesy of *House Beautiful*: pages 165–169; Timothy Hursley: pages 170–173.

Ricardo Legorreta, Rooms for the Spirit, *pages 174–185*
Mary F. Nichols: pages 174–177; Lourdes Legorreta: pages 178–185.

pages 186–187
Top row, left to right: Charles Correa; Robert Lautman; Peter Aaron/ESTO, courtesy of *House Beautiful*; Ron Parello; Lourdes Legorreta; Scott Frances, courtesy of *House Beautiful*.
Second row: A. Piovano and P. Albornoz; Tim Street–Porter; Jeff Goldberg/ESTO; Timothy Hursley.
Third row: Kari Haavisto, courtesy of *House Beautiful*; Timothy Hursley; Jeff Goldberg/ESTO; Jeremy Samuelson, courtesy of *House Beautiful*; Timothy Hursley, courtesy of *House Beautiful*.
Bottom row: John Vaughan, courtesy of *House Beautiful*; Mitsuo Matsuoka; Jeff Goldberg/ESTO; A. Piovano and P. Albornoz; Jeremy Samuelson, courtesy of *House Beautiful*; John Vaughan, courtesy of *House Beautiful*.